THIS ANNUAL BELONGS TO

PONY
magazine
ponymag.com

Published by
DJ Murphy (Publishers) Ltd,
Olive Studio, The Timber Yard,
Grange Road, Tilford, Farnham,
Surrey GU10 2DQ

**Who did what in PONY –
The Annual**
Contributors Kiera Boyle,
Sarah Burgess, Louise Kittle,
Nicky Moffatt, Megan Xavier-
Witherington
Senior Designer Adam Witt
Designers Lucy Claydon,
Paul Smail
Managing Director Zoe Cannon
Commercial Director Abi Cannon

Who took the pics
Photography Jon Stroud, arthorse,
nigel baker photography, Philip
Bird LRPS CPAGB, Aleksey Demin,
Sanit Fuangnakhon, Kento35,
Rita_Kochmarjova, kontrymphoto,
Marcin Kadziolka, Angela Lock,
Vladimir Tretyakov, Joe Turner, A.
Young photography, Makarova
Viktoria, StockphotoVideo, Zuzule
/shutterstock.com
Cover photo Jon Stroud
p96-97 Illustrations by Helena and
Rebecca Öhmark

PONY recommends you wear an
up-to-standard riding hat at all
times when mounted.

PONY magazine is published every
four weeks. To find out more about
PONY magazine, visit
ponymag.com
© Copyright DJ Murphy
(Publishers) Ltd 2023

Printed by
Printed in Italy by Rotolito S.p.A.

ISBN 978-1-913787-17-2

MIX
Paper from
responsible sources
FSC® C005461

RRP £12.99

INSIDE YOUR ANNUAL 2024

66

64

48

96

BOOST *your* CONFIDENCE...

Supercharge your self-belief and get ready to ace your next riding lesson!

RIDING IN A LESSON

If you've ever had a riding lesson and felt as if you're not good enough compared with the others in your group, or you're not meeting your instructor's expectations, you're not alone. Riding lessons can feel a bit like schoolwork, rather than fun, but, without them, you won't improve. So, here are four tips to give you the boost you need!

1 SET YOURSELF A GOAL

Spend time outside your lessons thinking about what you want to achieve – breaking it down into smaller goals as well as future aspirations – then talk to your instructor about your ideas. Putting a step-by-step plan in place to reach realistic goals is a sure-fire way to improve your skills and, ultimately, increase your confidence. The feeling when you've achieved your aims is like no other! Before your lesson, consider what mood you're in, too, and let your trainer know. This way you can manage expectations – it's okay to not always feel up for trying something new, so just be honest about it before you get started!

2 WORK ON YOUR MINDSET

Positivity is the key to success – being negative can lead to stress, increased emotions and decreased motivation, so try swapping negative words for positive ones. For example, instead of saying you can't do something, tell yourself you can and you'll be surprised at the outcome! One of the biggest pressures you'll face in a riding lesson is being the first one in your group to have a go at the exercise, but think realistically about the potential outcomes – nothing bad can happen from going first.

3 TALK TO YOUR INSTRUCTOR

Remember that your instructor is there to help you improve, learn and enjoy your time in the saddle! If you're unsure about something – such as how to tell if you're on the correct diagonal or what the aids are for leg-yield – just ask! You'll learn so much more by asking questions, so try to be brave. Remember, it's a good thing that you want to understand the task, rather than sitting quietly and hoping for the best. If you feel concerned about asking in front of others, why not chat to your instructor after the lesson?

4 TRACK YOUR PROGRESS

There's nothing more rewarding than seeing how far you've come in your riding journey! Keeping a diary or journal to monitor your progress is an awesome confidence-boosting technique – why not also get a pal to video your lessons so you can watch back the footage? You'll get to see your own progress first-hand!

TOUGH STUFF

Hooves are made of a really strong material called keratin – the same stuff that makes up your hair and nails! Keratin doesn't contain any nerve endings which is why ponies don't feel pain when they have their hooves trimmed and shoes put on. Arranged in horizontal layers to prevent excess damage, keratin creates a tough structure for your pony to stand on.

ALL ABOUT HOOVES

Learn loads of fantastic facts about your fave pony's feet!

TAKE YOUR TIME

Hooves grow very slowly and it can take 9–12 months for a pony to grow a whole new hoof! How quickly your pony's hoof wall grows depends on lots of different factors, such as his health status, diet, hoof quality and the weather. Hoof injuries can slow down the growing process, but making sure your pony's diet contains plenty of biotin, copper and zinc will help improve the quality of his hooves and, hopefully, reduce the risk of damage.

ROLE MODEL

Hooves have lots of different functions so it's really important we care for them because without good quality hooves, ponies can suffer from a variety of problems that affect their health and performance. Hooves carry the pony's weight, flex to absorb shock and protect joints, and they help circulate blood all the way up his legs. The frog is a flexible, triangular-shaped structure that plays a key role in shock absorption, but watch out – it's not made from keratin so is a very sensitive part of the foot!

TROUBLESOME TOES

Thousands of years ago, your pony's ancestors had three or four toes rather than just one hoof! Due to evolution and the changing climate and conditions they lived in, equines grew taller and heavier, so developed a single hoof to help them survive. Compared with multiple toes, hooves allow ponies to gallop away from predators faster!

TO SHOE OR NOT TO SHOE?

Ponies wear shoes to protect the sensitive parts of their feet and prevent them from being worn down quickly by rough surfaces. However, not all ponies need to wear shoes. Those with good conformation and hoof quality might be able to stay barefoot and, in recent years, keeping ponies barefoot has become more popular – even some top showjumpers have made the change from shod to barefoot!

HOOF CARE PRO

A farrier is the expert who cares for your pony's hooves by trimming and balancing them. He's also responsible for putting on your pony's shoes – unless he's barefoot! A pony should see the farrier every 6–8 weeks. If you're ever concerned about your pony's hooves, a farrier is the best person to ask for advice!

LET'S GO JOUSTING

Courage, bravery and speed – find out what it takes to joust

Welcome to the Middle Ages when jousting first began and knights used to learn practical hands-on horsemanship that provided them with a simulated practice for war. This quickly became a favourite sport that people loved to watch for entertainment.

DID YOU KNOW?

King Henry VIII had a severe leg injury when a horse fell on him during a tournament.

Jolly jousting

Jousting involves two knights being separated by a wooden panel. They charge at each other to try to knock the other contender off their horse onto the floor – ouch! They ride with a lance – a long pole used to push people off – and both knight and horse are dressed in armour as protection.

They used to aim to hit their opponent's chest, throat or helmet, but in later jousts, the rules were changed to hit the shield. Tournaments are won by knocking the opponent off their horse, gaining the most points or by completely breaking your lance – shattering the tip means max points!

DID YOU KNOW?

You had to be of noble lineage to be invited to a jousting tournament – how fancy!

Do you have what it takes?

To be a great knight and compete in jousting you must be...
- brave
- strong
- skillful
- respectful

The most common horse breeds used for jousting were...
- Andalusians
- Arabians
- Friesians
- Shires

Handy history

Jousting first started in 1066 and by the 14th century, knights were not the only ones drawn to playing this sport, with many members of the nobility joining in, including kings!

A wooden barrier was not always used during jousting and in the early days there was no divider – the competitors rode at each other head on. How crazy is that!

By the 16th century, the development of firearms put a stop to jousting, as there was no longer any need to use this skill on the battlefield. This caused competitive jousting to turn into a more choreographed routine for entertainment, rather than knights using it to perfect their skills.

DID YOU KNOW?

Jousting's still done today with a points system for different parts of the body, but players aren't allowed to knock their opponent off their horse.

DID YOU KNOW?

Tournaments were also used to win a lady's honour!

Keen knight

Excited to have a go at jousting? There are companies that run courses and lessons to train you to joust like a knight. But it doesn't stop there, as they give you the opportunity to dress up in medieval costume, too – how cool!

RIDE THE *perfect...* SHOWJUMPING ROUND

Smash your showjumping comp with our handy tips!

Flying high in the sky with your fave pony is so much fun, but when you go competing, you'll want to ride the perfect round to be in with a chance of bringing home a rosette! Here are six steps to help you do just that...

PICK UP THE PACE

You'll need to get your pony warmed up and in the zone before it's time for your round. Spend at least 10 minutes working him on the flat to get him supple and responsive before jumping him – you don't want to rush your warm-up and risk an injury!

By the end of your warm-up session your pony should be working actively and listening to your aids, so try different exercises before show day to find out how best to get him prepared.

Your canter for showjumping needs to be punchy and powerful, so ride lots of transitions within and between paces to get your pony focused on you and using his hindquarters. When it's time to pop some fences, keep them low to start with and try approaching the first few in trot to check your pony is in good balance and can maintain his rhythm.

TOP TIP
Watch a few people jump before it's your turn, so if they're having problems at a certain fence, you can plan how to ride it to avoid having the same issue!

ON FOOT
Walking the course is key to success, so make sure you arrive at your competition on time! As you walk around take note of any fences or areas of the course that might be tricky or spooky.

Counting the number of strides between doubles and related distances is essential so you can plan the line you'll ride. You won't be able to change the striding, but you can work out how you'll ride the distances – maybe you find there are four long strides for your pony between two fences, so you might decide to sit up and hold for five, instead.

STEP BY STEP

As you warm up and jump around the course, you'll come across a few different types of jumps. Cross-poles are a good starting point to warm up over because they encourage straightness and accuracy, so think about riding your pony towards the middle with an even rein contact and leg aids.

As you progress to uprights, allow your pony to canter actively, but avoid letting him rush towards the jump. If his canter is fast and flat, he'll be more likely to knock the fence, so think about using your leg to keep him up into your hand.

When it comes to jumping oxers, ask your pony for a slightly longer canter stride to allow him to open up and stretch over the fence more easily. Don't mistake this with going fast – think impulsion, not speed! Encourage him with your legs, but half-halt to keep the rhythm.

TOP TIP
When you enter the arena, ride past any fences you think your pony might find spooky before the bell goes. This allows him to look at them and realise they're not so spooky after all.

The key thing to remember when riding through combinations is to remain in a light seat

COOL COMBOS

Depending on what level you're competing at you're sure to find one or two combinations in your showjumping course, and they'll either be in the form of doubles (two fences one or two strides apart) or trebles (three fences in a row). The key thing to remember when riding through combinations is to remain in a light seat, but keep your upper body tall. Leaning forward or sitting deep in the saddle means your pony will struggle to maintain momentum and pick up his feet quickly for the next fence.

As you approach and ride through the combination, keep your pony straight by channelling him between your hand and legs. Be sure to look up at something that's past the final fence, too!

TOP TIP
As you fold, think about pushing your hips towards the back of the saddle and allowing with your hands. Try not to throw your upper body forwards as this will put your pony off balance. Getting left behind will also impact your pony's way of going, so aim to keep your body flexible so you can go with his movements.

BETWEEN THE ELEMENTS

How you land and get away from one fence will influence your approach to the next. So, stay reactive to your pony's movements by sitting lightly in the saddle and encouraging him on with your leg to help maintain his rhythm and balance – doing this will help you nail the approach to the next jump!

Be sure to use all the space you have between fences and ride the line you set out to. Wonky lines and tight turns will likely lead to a loss of rhythm and even a refusal or run out.

SPEED AND STYLE

Lots of showjumping courses are two-phase, which means if you jump the first phase clear you ride straight into the jump-off. Whether or not they're separate, they're tonnes of fun to ride, but all too often riders make silly mistakes that cost them the win!

When walking the jump-off section of the course, think about where you can save time. You may be able to push your pony on, or find some corners to cut and fences you can jump on an angle. Carefully choose which corners you cut, though, because turning too tightly might mean your pony can't see the fence in time. It's also best to avoid rushing your pony around a jump off because it could cause his canter to become flat which means he might knock fences.

GET GROOMING

Follow our step-by-step guide to achieving the perfect groom

Grooming's an important part of daily pony care because it keeps your pony's skin and coat in good condition, stimulates blood flow and gives you the chance to check him over for any lumps, bumps or cuts that might need attention. Here's how to do it...

1 FOOT FIRST

Always start by picking out your pony's feet to remove any mud or bedding. Using the pointy end of your hoof pick, work your way down from heel to toe, avoiding his sensitive frog. Brush any excess mud off and if your pony wears shoes, check they're not loose or twisted.

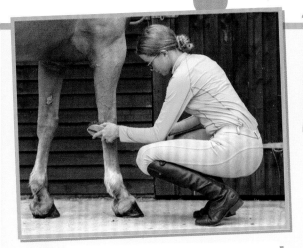

2 BANISH MUD

If your pony's muddy, allow the mud to dry then use a dandy brush – the hard bristled one – in short back-and-forth motions to get rid of it. Remember that the tough bristles can be uncomfy on clipped or sensitive skin, or bony areas, so stick to using it on your pony's legs and unclipped coat.

4 MOVE YOUR BODY

To remove fine dust and loose dirt from your pony's coat, grab a soft-bristled body brush and use in long, sweeping motions. It's a good idea to start at your pony's head – you can buy special face brushes that are smaller and easier to use – and work your way along his body, finishing off with his legs.

5 LOVELY LOCKS

Grab a mane and tail comb and some detangling spray to make your pony's locks knot-free. Stand to the side of him, hold his tail in one hand and spray the detangler with the other. Then brush one small section at a time and finish off by working your way through his mane and forelock.

3 MOULTING MASTER

A curry comb is the ultimate tool when it comes to moulting season! Use it in gentle, circular motions all over your pony's body and watch all the loose hair and dirt come out – it's sooo satisfying.

6 SPARKLE AND SHINE

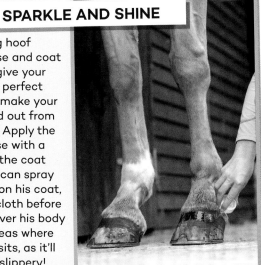

Using hoof grease and coat shine will give your groom the perfect finish and make your pony stand out from the crowd. Apply the hoof grease with a brush. For the coat shine, you can spray it directly on his coat, or onto a cloth before wiping it over his body – avoid areas where your tack sits, as it'll make him slippery!

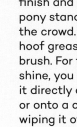

TOP TIP
Hot-clothing your pony is a great way to get rid of stubborn dust and scurf without bathing him. Simply dampen a cloth (or sponge!) with hand-hot water and rub all over his body!

HIGHLAND PONIES

Get to know this super-sweet breed...

One of the three native pony breeds of Scotland (the other two being Shetlands and Eriskays), the Highland pony has adapted over many centuries. Their winter coats are strong and dense to help them survive the cold, harsh winters of Scotland. Although they seem hard and tough on the outside, these cute ponies have a very kind nature.

DID YOU KNOW?

Highland ponies don't usually grow bigger than 14.2hh but are no smaller than 13hh.

Travel back in time

In the 1880s, the Highland pony was originally a small horse used by farmers. They horses did all the work, from being used as pack animals to a form of transportation and they also pulled carts.

Moving on in time to the 1950s when pony trekking began in Scotland, Highland ponies showed they are the perfect breed for this activity, as they have such a quiet nature and can carry heavy weights.

BREED BIO

Highland ponies...
- ✓ are stocky but well balanced
- ✓ have incredibly strong legs
- ✓ possess good-shaped feet
- ✓ have short ears
- ✓ show bright friendly eyes
- ✓ come in a wide range of shades mostly commonly grey. You can also find black, bays and chestnuts.
- ✓ are a heavy breed for their size, weighing up to 550kg!

Why the Highland pony?

Today Highlands are used for all kinds of riding and driving activities. They're very popular for showing but are also keen jumpers! Using the Highland pony for these activities comes down to their personality, though – they're very calm, steady ponies, but in no way lazy, making them perfect for getting the job done under pressure.

What does it take to show a Highland pony?

When showing a Highland pony, you don't need to plait, pull or trim the mane, tail and feathers. However, during winter they can be clipped for their welfare. White markings are not permitted in the show ring apart from a small white star. Any excessive hair, for example under their chins, should be wetted with water to make it look neat and tidy. Hooves should be well oiled, too!

FUN FACT

Lots of Highlands have primitive markings, many having an eel stripe down their spine and even zebra stripes on the insides of their legs!

DID YOU KNOW?

Based on a Celtic pony type, the Highland pony has had many genetic additions from other breeds, including Clydesdale, Spanish and, most recently in the 19th century, Arab.

BIRTHDAY TEA PARTY

Celebrate your pony's special day with an adorable picnic!

You'll need...

- [ ] bread
- [ ] your fave sandwich filling
- [ ] pony-shaped cutters
- [ ] carrots, apples and pears
- [ ] digestive biscuits
- [ ] icing pens
- [ ] unicorn cupcake kit

Ask an adult for help when using a knife and the oven

1 Follow the instructions on your cupcake kit to bake and decorate them.

2 Grab your icing pens and decorate the biscuits with lots of different pony designs!

3 Make your sandwiches and use a cutter to create pony shapes!

4 Cut your fruit and veg into long strips so you can share them with your fave pony!

5 Grab a picnic blanket, plates and party hats. Then blow up some balloons.

6 Set up your tea party near your pony's field and bring some friends along to celebrate his big day!

WORK ON YOUR WALK

Ever wondered how to make the most of your pony's walk? Here's what you need to know

If you think walking's boring, think again! Not only is walk an important part of any dressage test, but it can do wonders for your pony's muscle development and help you get him super-tuned into your aids – cool, huh? Here's our guide to walking like a pro. There's nothing you can't do in this pace!

Fancy footwork
Walk is a four-beat pace and the footfall sequence is...
- outside hindleg
- outside foreleg
- inside hindleg
- inside foreleg

POSITION PERFECT
As with any gait, keeping a good position in the saddle will help you get the best out of your pony's walk, so think about...
- looking up and straight ahead
- keeping your elbows soft – imagine your forearms are an extension of your reins with your thumbs on top
- having relaxed legs that hang down by your pony's sides, with your heels slightly lower than your toes

TOP TIP
To ride a half-halt, apply your leg to keep the energy, then gently squeeze your outside rein to rebalance your pony's body.

EXERCISE ONE

ON AND BACK

Did you know your pony has more than one walk? As well as his normal walk, which is known as a medium pace, you can ask him to shorten his steps (collected walk) or lengthen them (extended walk). So next time you're out hacking or schooling in an arena, why not have a go at riding the different walk 'gears'?

1. Start by asking your pony to shorten his walk strides by making some tiny half-halts on the reins, using your legs to keep the rhythm.
2. Ride a few steps of collected walk until you feel your pony lighten his forehand and become lighter in the rein contact.
3. Next, lengthen your reins a little so your pony can stretch his head and neck forwards and use your leg and seat aids to ask him to take some longer steps.
4. Keep riding between the 'gears', seeing how smoothly you can make your transitions from one to the other.

EXERCISE TWO

HANDY HILLWORK

If you have access to hills or inclines on one of your hacking routes, why not use them to improve your pony's walk? Believe it or not, walking up and down hills will give your pony a full body workout without putting too much stress on his limbs – and you'll increase his fitness levels, too! Make sure you keep your pony straight, so his hindlegs follow in the line of his forelegs. If he's crooked, your hillwork won't be half as effective!

Fix it - fast!

If your pony tries to jog when you ask him to walk (ponies just looove doing that!), try to stay relaxed, allow with your hand and sit deeply into the saddle so your body moves with him!

THE MIDNIGHT STABLES

Dezzie's on the brink of selling her pony, Bean, until she takes a magical trip that changes her life for ever

'Why do I bother?' thought Dezzie, as her schooling session ended in tears yet again. Her pony, Bean, had tossed her head in the air, napped and refused to move, as usual. Although Dezzie had resisted her parents' suggestion that perhaps Bean would be better suited to a different home, she was starting to believe they might be right.

Bean was Dezzie's first pony and, when the family had bought her a year earlier, they hadn't really known what they were looking for. They'd ended up with a fiery, inexperienced young mare, who'd turned into a nightmare. Dezzie had had countless lessons, and had fallen off so many times that she was losing her confidence. They'd had Bean checked for everything possible, too, consulting the vet, saddle fitter and physio, but there appeared to be no health-related causes for Bean's behaviour. To make things worse, Bean always went well when Dezzie's instructor, Kerry, was riding her. All in all, it made Dezzie feel like a terrible rider.

A trip down memory lane

So, that was it. Bean's 'for sale' advert was put in the equine classifieds that evening. But for some reason, Dezzie still had a voice in her head asking, 'But what if you're making the wrong decision?'

The following morning, Dezzie was grooming Bean, who seemed to be enjoying the attention. Why couldn't she be that sweet all the time? Bean snorted and Dezzie felt her stomach churn. She'd made her decision and couldn't go back on it – right?

As Dezzie closed the stable door and headed to the tack room, she suddenly tripped, and it sent her hurtling towards the ground. She hit her head on the concrete floor and everything went black.

Dezzie groaned and sat up, feeling her forehead. To her surprise, it didn't hurt. 'That's strange,' she thought as she rubbed her eyes and looked around.

She appeared to be at the yard, except it was night and everything had a dark blue glow with mist swirling around it. As she stood up and walked through the barn, she didn't recognise any of the ponies standing in the stables and they looked blurry, like holograms. 'What's going on?' she wondered.

> *Everything had a dark blue glow with mist swirling around*

Endless possibilities

Just then, Dezzie heard footsteps coming towards her and she held her breath. Who could it be? It was someone she instantly recognised – her instructor, Kerry. "Welcome, Dezzie," Kerry said in a calm tone.

"Kerry? Where are we?" asked Dezzie.

"We're at the Midnight Stables, of course," Kerry replied matter of factly.

"The where?" Dezzie said, confused.

"This is the magic part of your brain you can come to whenever you feel lost. Yours exists in the form of your yard – your happy place," explained Kerry. "I will be your guide – but I've taken the form of your riding instructor to help you feel more comfortable. I have lots to show you. Take a peek into the stables. Do any of these ponies take your fancy?"

Dezzie walked past the row of ponies, admiring them all one by one, each totally different from the last. "They're yours," said Kerry. "Or at least, they are in different versions of your life."

Totally confused now, Dezzie stared in wonder.

"These are all memories," Kerry continued. "And they're stored here at the Midnight Stables. Take one of the ponies for a ride and see what happens. If you find one you want to keep, you'll stay in that version of your life. But if at any point you find yourself regretting your decision, you'll return here."

Nervous, but a little excited, Dezzie was drawn to the door of an athletic-looking grey Welsh pony. His name plate read 'Gandalf'. As Dezzie entered the stable, she was transported to another life.

Finding the right fit

The sensation of being dropped into an alternate reality was bizarre. Dezzie's brain was suddenly filled with knowledge she didn't know she had, and she recognised people, although they were all slightly different in some way. She found herself with Gandalf on loan. Dezzie was shocked at how much more confident a rider she was in this life and, over a few weeks, she attended Pony Club rallies and went cross-country schooling – things she'd only dreamt of doing before.

Gandalf was awesome – dependable, forward and brave. But things took a turn when, one day, Dezzie and her parents had a call saying that Gandalf's owner wanted him back. The feeling of despair Dezzie felt as she watched him loading onto the lorry was so heartbreaking that she felt herself fading away.

Suddenly, she was back at the Midnight Stables. "Not quite what you were after, then?" said Kerry.

Dezzie shook her head. "No, I never want a pony that can be taken away from me," she replied.

Kerry nodded and gestured towards a tall bay sport pony called Hugo. Dezzie opened his door.

Time and time again

In this new life, Dezzie was an excellent rider. She was serious about her goals and attended affiliated dressage and showjumping competitions with Hugo and won – it was immense. Surely this was the life she was meant to have? But one day, Hugo came in from the field very lame. After examinations and

tests, the vet said it was unlikely that Hugo could ever be ridden again. Dezzie loved Hugo dearly but found herself back at the Midnight Stables for a third time.

Desperate to find her forever horse, Dezzie ran towards another stable. And another. And another. Each time, something happened that caused her to feel a twinge of regret or longing for her old life. She was running out of ponies. Maybe she wasn't destined to have a pony at all?

But as she approached the final stable, she gasped. Bean! She'd been there all along! A tear welled in Dezzie's eye and Kerry placed a hand on her shoulder. "Go on," Kerry said, smiling.

As Dezzie touched the door bolt, she felt an electric current surge through her and a vision shot across her eyes like a film. She then saw herself. She was much older and she was hugging Bean, who had a red, winner's sash around her neck. She saw blissful hacks on Bean through the countryside and then she was laughing with friends at pairs cross-country. A feeling of pride coursed through her body, knowing she'd truly earned it. The Midnight Stables was showing her the future with Bean.

Back down to earth

"Dezzie? Dezzie?" She opened her eyes to be met with a very worried-looking Mum cradling her head. "Oh, thank goodness!" she said as Dezzie woke up. "You must've fallen and hit your head."

"How long have I been out?" Dezzie asked, feeling as if she'd been gone for months.

"Only a few seconds," said Kerry – the real one this time. Suddenly, it all flooded back.

"Bean!" Dezzie shouted as she jumped to her feet. "We have to take down her advert right now! I'm going to improve."

Dezzie turned to Bean and said, "You're my forever horse and I believe in us – I know we'll get there."

And, of course, eventually, that's exactly what they did.

IN HIS SHOES

Eight awesome activities to do with your pony that'll make him feel fab

Have you ever considered what your pony's thinking, how he feels or what he likes and dislikes? Ponies thrive on food, freedom and friends, so any activity that involves at least one of these things is sure to make him happy. Why not treat him to these eight activities and see for yourself how much he enjoys them?

1

Whether you've got some time to kill, your pony's stuck on box rest or has restricted access to turnout because of the weather, taking him for a graze in-hand on a patch of yummy grass is sure to brighten up his day. Most ponies will enjoy extra time in the field, too, but check it's OK with your yard manager first.

2

Giving your pony a scratch or massaging him with a curry comb on his fave itchy spot will make him feel sooo relaxed. Not sure where that spot is? Try his withers, chest or behind his ears!

3

If you love exploring with your pony, this one's for you. Taking him on a hack to his favourite stretch of grass for a gallop or down to the river for a splash will make his ears prick forward with delight!

4

Ponies love socialising with their pals, so treat yours to time with his equine BFF. Why not let them groom each other on the yard, or take them for a ride together?

5

Foraging through hedgerows for tasty snacks will not only make your pony happy, it's great for his diet and mental wellbeing, too. An extra treat every now and again won't hurt – but don't get too carried away, as it won't be good for his waistline!

6

There's no doubt your pony will love an extra day off from his exercise routine, especially if it means he gets a few more hours in the field with food and friends! Instead, you could spend the time watching him and getting to know him better – it'll boost your bond loads!

7

Treating your pony to a physio appointment is the ultimate way to get him feeling relaxed, refreshed and ready to take on his next challenge! They'll work to loosen up his muscles, so he'll be on top form when you get back on board.

8

Watching your freshly bathed pony roll in a muddy patch might be your worst nightmare, and he'll probably look pleased with himself for turning into a mud monster, but he'll love the feeling of freedom it'll give him.

WHAT'S YOUR WORKPLACE?

Which horsey career would best suit you? We're here to help you find out

There are tons of jobs involving horses, but have you ever wondered which one you'd most like to do? If so, you've come to the right place. From farriers to physiotherapists and grooms to professional riders, we've got it all covered. Take our quiz to find out what your future could hold.

1

Your favourite subjects at school are...

- ○ **a.** English and other languages
- ○ **b.** Science and maths
- ○ **c.** PE
- ○ **d.** Art and design

2

When it comes to spending time with your fave pony, you most enjoy...

- ○ **a.** Giving him a bath and thorough groom
- ○ **b.** Taking his temperature, pulse and respiration to check he's healthy
- ○ **c.** Riding and training him
- ○ **d.** Mucking out, poo picking and cleaning his tack

3

You're helping to organise a show at your yard. What role do you take on?

- ○ **a.** Writing the schedule and publicising the event on social media
- ○ **b.** Health and safety, making sure there's an experienced support team in place in case anything goes wrong
- ○ **c.** Writing or stewarding for the judge on the day, in between competing there yourself – of course
- ○ **d.** Setting up the rings and mend any broken equipment ready for show day

4

Your fave pony is very slightly lame and you think he might have tweaked something in the field. How are you feeling?

- ○ **a.** Upset. When you get home you email PONY Mag's Help! pages for advice
- ○ **b.** Concerned, but determined to do everything you can to get him right
- ○ **c.** Annoyed. You know your pony will be okay, but two days before a comp – argh!
- ○ **d.** Intrigued. Before you call the vet, you have a good look over your pony to see if you can find anything

5

Your friends would describe you as being...

- ○ **a.** Creative and meticulous
- ○ **b.** Clever and caring
- ○ **c.** Determined and hard-working
- ○ **d.** Practical and physically strong

6

You go to meet your bestie's new pony. What's the first thing you do?

- ○ **a.** Take loads of photos and ask her all about him
- ○ **b.** Check him over and look at his conformation
- ○ **c.** Ask her to tack him up so you can watch him being ridden
- ○ **d.** Tell her he looks like a good sort, after having a look at him from all angles

7

You've got £50 birthday money. What do you do with it?

- ○ **a.** Spend it on horsey books and renew your subscription to PONY
- ○ **b.** Put it to one side in case your pony needs something
- ○ **c.** Book a couple of riding lessons
- ○ **d.** Use it to buy materials to do a PONY Annual make!

8

When it comes to social media, you...

- ○ **a.** Update your status or story every hour
- ○ **b.** Use it mostly for research and learning more about ponies
- ○ **c.** Go on YouTube to watch videos of professional riders
- ○ **d.** Aren't really interested and haven't got time for it. You'd rather show your creativity in another way

9

Your ideal pony is...

- ○ **a.** An absolute beauty with looks that dazzle everyone
- ○ **b.** One who's in good health. You're not fussed about looks or talent, as long as he's okay
- ○ **c.** Full of scope, athletic and oozing talent
- ○ **d.** A practical sort who can do a bit of everything

10

Your friend asks if he can borrow your pony for a fun ride. What do you say?

- ○ **a.** Of course, but you'd like to come along and take videos on the day
- ○ **b.** You say yes, but give him a long list of dos and don'ts – you don't want your pony to come to any harm
- ○ **c.** You would say yes, but you're already doing the fun ride on your pony, so sadly he can't
- ○ **d.** Yeah sure. You can come along and help if he wants.

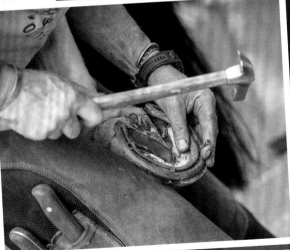

How did you get on? Check out p101 for the answers!

BOOST your CONFIDENCE...

RIDING ALONE

Determined to ride on your own but nervous at the idea? Here are four fab tips to help!

Schooling or hacking alone might be something new to you if you learnt to ride at a riding school, and the thought of riding without someone on the ground to guide and help you can be daunting. But with our confidence-boosting tips you'll banish the nerves and have so many more awesome riding sessions!

1 STAY SAFE

Always wear a riding hat that's up to standard whenever you're in the saddle. When riding alone, you might choose to wear a body protector, too, for an extra confidence boost. If you're hacking by yourself, make sure you're wearing at least one item of high-vis – and your pony as well– so you're extra visible. It's a good idea to let your yard manager know where you're going and what time you'll be back, and always take a charged phone with you in case of an emergency.

2 MAKE A PLAN

Planning what your riding session will involve is the best way to make it enjoyable – plus, it'll be really productive! Before you ride, set out your goal and think about how you can achieve it. It could be as simple as practising changing the rein, or riding for five circuits without stirrups. Whatever your target, the feeling once you've achieved it will be awesome. Imagining you're in a lesson is another great way to build your confidence – it can help keep your position in check, too!

3 KEEP THINGS SIMPLE

The best thing to do while riding by yourself is to stick to your comfort zone. Keep your session simple by riding an exercise you've done a few times before – one that you feel confident doing. Build things up slowly and don't ask too much of your pony if you're not sure of his reaction. There's no need to rush or try something new every time you ride – you can be pushed out of your comfort zone in your lessons!

4 GET TALKING

Whether you're going for a solo adventure or practising your flatwork moves in the school, talking to your pony is a great way to boost your confidence. You might talk to him for company, or perhaps it'll help distract you from the negative thoughts whirring around in your head. Rewarding your pony with your voice is sure to help settle him and improve his trust in you, too.

ALL ABOUT TUMMIES

A super-interesting and extra-large structure, find out more about your pony's digestive system!

EAT LIKE A HORSE

Ponies are herbivores which means they only eat plant material and their diets are largely made up of lots of roughage, such as hay and grass. Thousands of years ago, equines lived on soft fruits and leaves but as the world's climate changed, their digestive systems evolved to cope with a high-forage diet.

TUMMY ACHE

Ponies should be fed little and often to help keep their guts healthy and working efficiently. If a pony's stomach is empty, the acid can splash onto the stomach lining and cause ulcers, which are really painful. Saliva helps to neutralise stomach acid but it's only produced when chewing, which is part of the reason why ponies need an almost constant supply of food! Symptoms of gastric ulcers include sudden weight loss, sensitive girth area and changes in behaviour, coat and body condition – if you think your pony might be suffering from ulcers, ask your vet for advice.

START TO FINISH

The digestive system, also known as the gastrointestinal tract, is a very large structure that's split into the foregut and the hindgut. Each section has several elements that have different roles in the process of breaking down food. On average, the whole process of digestion – from mouth to manure – can take 36–72 hours! Wow!

BLOCKED UP

Colic is when a pony experiences gut pain and this can be caused by lots of different things, such as stress or abrupt changes in diet. Dietary adjustments should be made slowly, otherwise the bacteria may struggle to break down the food, leading to a blockage. If your pony doesn't drink enough water, the food might get stuck, which is very painful. Lack of appetite and frequently looking at his sides are some of the symptoms of colic – if you suspect your pony has colic, call the vet immediately.

BREAK IT DOWN

The hindgut consists of the caecum, large and small colons and the rectum. Ponies are known as hindgut fermenters because, in the hindgut, there are millions of bacteria and microbes that are responsible for breaking down the fibre in feed – because ponies' diets are fibre-based, it's really important to make sure the hindgut stays healthy!

IN THE BEGINNING

The foregut is made up of the mouth, oesophagus, stomach and small intestine. Food starts in the mouth where it's chewed, then it's swallowed and passed down through the oesophagus – this muscular structure only works in one direction, which means ponies can't throw up! The food then travels through the stomach and into the small intestine, and that's where many of the nutrients are absorbed.

AWESOME ARCHERY

Ready, steady, aim... learn all about mounted archery

Have you ever wondered what it would be like to canter along on your fave pony and shoot an arrow at the same time? Same here! Horse archery, also known as mounted archery, is super-cool and requires tons of skill – so, let's find out more about this awesome sport!

DID YOU KNOW?

Archers wear a bracer (arm guard) to protect the surface of their bow-holding arm.

What's involved in archery?

Mounted archery involves an archer riding past targets, which the rider then shoots at using a bow and arrow.

In modern-day mounted archery, the track can range from 60m to 150m in length (depending on the competition) with barriers either side of this track to keep the horse straight. Each rider has a certain number of runs for shooting at the targets and all runs must be done at a canter or gallop! The run is timed and if you take too long, you can receive a time penalty – so you've got to keep your pony moving!

Do you have what it takes?

To be an epic mounted archer you need...
- bravery
- horsemanship skills
- good balance
- accuracy

Typical breeds used for mounted archery include...
- Thoroughbreds
- Quarter Horses
- Akhal-Tekes
  Any breed can be good for mounted archery as long as they are introduced to it properly and are ultra-brave!

Heaps of history

Mounted archery first appeared in the Iron Age, when it was used for hunting animals for food and also in battle to assist on-foot archers. By the 16th century, mounted archery was no longer needed, as the first firearms had been invented and these had a longer range compared with bows and arrows. Today, mounted archery is a competitive sport.

DID YOU KNOW?

Mounted archery first appeared in the 9th century BC and was used by the Assyrian army who lived in the Middle East.

Why not have a go?

You've already got the riding part in the bag but, don't worry, you'll learn archery from the ground before you start trying to ride and shoot! If your pony's feeling brave, why not get in touch with a local mounted archery club and attend a training day? Some clubs even have ponies trained for you to learn on. Who knows? Maybe one day you'll be on Team GB!

DID YOU KNOW?

The British Horseback Archery Association (BHAA) is the official body for the sport. Visit bhaa.org.uk

RIDE THE *perfect...* CROSS-COUNTRY ROUND

You'll be a cross-country champion with our top tips!

Cruising around a cross-country course is a totally awesome feeling but you're sure to be challenged along the way! So, get ready to tackle the terrain and soar over skinnies with our XC tips.

A WARM WELCOME

As you warm up for your cross-country round, focus on getting your pony moving forwards in a positive, punchy canter. You're sure to have your straightness and accuracy tested while out on course, so check that your pony is listening to your aids and you have good control – this is especially important when there are lots of other ponies around in the warm-up.

Practise shortening and lengthening his strides and choose an inviting fence, such as a log or house, to warm up over. These types of fence are the ones that can save you time on course because you can approach in a more forward canter, compared to a skinny that requires lots of precision, for example. So have a go at this in your warm up to get yourself tuned in and ready for an epic round!

GO ZOOMIES

One of the best things about going XC is getting to gallop through the countryside with your pony! Not only is it tonnes of fun, but pushing on between fences will help you achieve the optimum time, too – although, if your pony is super-speedy you might not want to encourage him on too much, otherwise you could get penalised for being too fast!

By bringing yourself out of the saddle into two-point position, your pony will be able to open up his stride and cover more ground. But be sure to practise riding in light seat while training at home because it's hard work!

TOP TIP
Wearing a stopwatch on the cross-country course can help you avoid getting any time faults for being too fast or slow! Checking out the minute markers while you're walking the course will give you a good idea of the pace you'll need.

BLANK SPACE

Ponies often find ditches spooky because they don't really understand what they are, so they might stop to look at them before leaping over. But your ditch-jumping success is all down to how you set up your pony on the approach. Your pony's unable to see directly in front of and below him, so allowing with your reins slightly and encouraging him to drop his head and neck a few strides away means he will be able to see it in plenty of time. Think about keeping your leg on and sitting up tall to avoid throwing your pony off balance, and focus on having a soft, supple position so you easily follow his movements.

FIND YOUR LINE

Jumping skinnies is a true test of accuracy! Some riders find them tricky because the risk of a run out is much greater with less jump to aim for, but you don't need to ride them differently to any other fence so try not to be nervous just because they're narrower.

On your approach, think about keeping your pony in a steady, balanced canter by using a half halt. Ride your pony towards the middle of the jump by keeping him super-straight with your hands and legs – maintain an even rein contact, look up and over the jump and widen your hands slightly to create a channel for him to go through. If you find your pony drifts to one side, close your rein towards his wither and press with your leg to push him back onto a straight line.

UP AND DOWN

Jumping up steps is very similar to jumping a normal fence – all you have to remember is to keep yourself out of the saddle slightly because the landing phase is different.

However, when it comes to steps down there's a little more to think about. As with ditches, your pony needs to be given the chance to see the obstacle in front of him, so on your approach lengthen your reins slightly to encourage him to drop his head. If your pony's head is too high, he's likely to over jump so think about keeping your upper body tilted back slightly and pushing your lower leg forward for extra stability. It's a good idea to bring your pony back to walk for the first few times you jump down steps to give him confidence, but whatever pace you're approaching in remember to lengthen your reins as he drops down so he can freely move his head and neck.

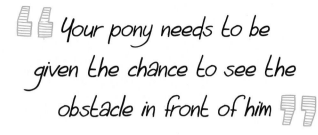

Your pony needs to be given the chance to see the obstacle in front of him

SPLASHING AROUND

Water complexes can be really exciting for ponies if they love getting their toes wet, but for others they can be scary – after all, they won't know how deep it is and light reflections can change the appearance in the blink of an eye! Take your time during training to really build your pony's confidence with water. Yes, there are more benefits to puddles than you first thought!

If your pony isn't keen on water, avoid letting him come back to walk while out on course as this will give him more time to shy away. It's a good idea to bring him back to trot, though, and use your voice and leg aids to encourage him through.

TOP TIP
When it's time for your round, you'll be called over to the start box then given a countdown before setting off. So, listen carefully to the steward and be prepared to go by riding lots of transitions around the start box to keep your pony focused.

BATHING BREAKDOWN

Get your pony sparkling clean from head to toe with our bathing guide

Bathing your fave pony is so much fun and there's nothing better than seeing him gleam in the sunshine. So, whether you're off to a comp, preparing him for a clip or just think he needs a thorough wash, here's how to do it...

1 SOAK IT UP

First, get your pony's coat wet using the hose or a bucket of water and a sponge. If it's a chilly day, it's a good idea to use warm water if you have access to it or wash his body in sections, rather than all in one go, to avoid him getting cold.

BUBBLE TIME

2 There are two options for applying shampoo to your pony – you can either squeeze some into a bucket and bubble it up, or apply it directly onto his coat. Both ways are really effective, but you might find you go through a lot more shampoo putting it directly on your pony.

MOULTING MASTER

4 You can apply shampoo to his mane and tail in the same way as you did his body – work through with your fingers, making sure you get all the way down to the hair roots. If you want to apply a conditioner, rinse his mane and tail thoroughly to get rid of the shampoo, then work the product in and brush through using a comb.

SQUEAKY CLEAN

3 Using a sponge, curry comb or your hands, thoroughly work the shampoo into your pony's coat. Avoid getting the bubbles near your pony's eyes because it might make him irritable, then work your way along his body and down his legs.

WASH AWAY

5 The most important step of the bathing process is rinsing off. Be sure to wash off all bubbles because dried shampoo can be uncomfy on your pony's skin and cause irritation. It's easiest to use a hose for this step so you can rinse his whole body thoroughly.

TOP TIP

Pop a rug on your pony when you're done to keep him warm and help him dry. If it's a sunny day you could take him for a graze in-hand – he'll love the extra snacks!

SCRAPE OFF

6 To remove excess water from your pony's body, use a sweat scraper and apply a small amount of pressure, moving it in the direction of his coat. You can use a towel, too, to help specific areas dry quickly.

COAT OF MANY *colours*

Did you know your fave pony colour can tell you a lot about your own personality? Try our quiz to find out how

Whether you'd choose a chestnut, bagsy a bay, go gooey about a grey or drool over a dun, your fave pony colour says a lot about you. Have a go at our fun quiz to discover how your dream colour choice can reveal a lot of personality traits you never even knew you had!

1 **When it comes to grooming and bathing your fave pony, you...**

○ **a.** can't get enough of it. There aren't enough hours in the day for you to make him look sparkling clean

○ **b.** don't mind washing a few white socks and giving him the once over, but you don't want to spend hours doing it

○ **c.** just clean the areas where his tack might rub, such as under the saddle and around his face

○ **d.** enjoy the bathing process but love nothing more than seeing the sun reflect on his coat afterwards

2 **Your fave equine movie star is...**

○ **a.** Mystic
○ **b.** Pilgrim from *Horse Whisperer*
○ **c.** Black Beauty
○ **d.** Spirit

3 **When turning your pony out in the field, you like to...**

○ **a.** rug him from head to toe, put on turnout boots and pop him in the driest paddock on the yard

○ **b.** use an appropriate rug and wash his legs off when he comes in

○ **c.** only rug him if you need to, as you love watching him wallow in the mud

○ **d.** keep his coat clean with a rug and be thankful he has dark legs

4 You go shopping for matchy-matchy gear for your fave pony and buy...

- a. every colour you can afford
- b. brown
- c. anything bright and blingy - the more diamantes, the better
- d. blue or green

5 Pick your fave breed of pony from our list...

- a. Connemara
- b. Haflinger
- c. Friesian
- d. Fjord

6 When you go outside, you most like to see...

- a. snow
- b. autumn leaves
- c. stars in the night sky
- d. sunshine

7 You'd most love to...

- a. have a go at the high-level dressage movements at the Spanish Riding School on a Lipizzaner
- b. work in the forest, using Suffolk Punch horses to pull heavy loads
- c. have a go at jousting and being a knight on an Andalusian or Friesian
- d. visit a ranch and ride cowboy style on an American Quarter Horse

8 Your favourite ice cream flavour is...

- a. vanilla
- b. salted caramel
- c. Oreo
- d. butterscotch

9 You're signing up for an art class after school. Which one attracts you most?

- a. Minimalist painting
- b. Watercolours
- c. Sketching with charcoal
- d. Ceramics

10 Your ideal holiday would include...

- a. skiing
- b. long walks through the countryside
- c. Seeing the Northern Lights
- d. lying on a beach

How did you get on? Check out p101 for the answers!

EXMOOR PONIES

Get to know this super-strong breed...

DID YOU KNOW?

Every year there's a round-up of the Exmoor ponies on the moor known as a 'gathering'. This is when the ponies have a health check.

Although Exmoor ponies are ultra-cute and cuddly, they're very hardy and are able to adapt to cold weather and grow thick coats to keep them dry and warm through winter. This is great for some of the semi-feral Exmoors roaming free in a large area of Devon and Somerset, as they don't need to rely on being rugged up in the harsher winters.

Marching on in time

The Exmoor pony has lived alongside man for nearly 30,000 years. They have helped contribute to the evolution of farming, by ploughing and carrying materials to markets. Today, the Exmoor pony is more commonly used for riding all kinds of activities, while the free-living herds carry on roaming the moors of Devon.

It wasn't always plain sailing for the ponies, though. The late 1940s saw Exmoor ponies almost becoming extinct when owners went away to war and the ponies played a big part in helping with pulling and carrying equipment for the soldiers.

Exmoor ponies belong to the mountain and moorland pony breeds native to the British Isles. They're said to be the pony that most closely resembles the first wild horse. How cool is that!

BREED BIO

Exmoor ponies...
- ☑ are 11.2–12.3hh
- ☑ can weigh up to 370kg
- ☑ boast a thick mane and tail
- ☑ have mealy markings around the eyes, muzzle and flanks
- ☑ have tough feet
- ☑ can be bay, brown and dun
- ☑ have small ears
- ☑ are stocky and powerful

FUN FACT

There is evidence to suggest that the Exmoor is Britain's oldest pony breed.

DID YOU KNOW?

After the Second World War, there were only 50 Exmoor ponies left!

Why are they great first ponies?

Exmoors are very kind, trustworthy and hardworking, which makes them the best first pony to learn to ride on. They're also quick learners, so are willing to try everything you throw their way! Whether it's being a lead-rein pony or being a jumping superstar, they are sure to try their absolute best. Don't be fooled by their small stature, though. They're incredibly strong and can carry small adults, so you won't need to worry about outgrowing them too quickly!

Make! VALENTINE'S CUSHION

Make the perfect pony present for someone special

1 Download and print the templates, then fold your pieces of fabric in half and cut out the heart template.

2 Cut out the horse shape from the black felt and sew (or use fabric glue to stick) it onto one of the hearts.

3 Place the two heart shapes back to back so the insides are facing outwards. Sew them together with a running stitch about 5mm in from the edge.

You'll need...

- [ ] black felt
- [ ] two pieces of fabric, no smaller than 30x40cm
- [ ] cushion or soft toy filling
- [ ] sewing kit
- [ ] templates

Download the template at bit.ly/VALENTINES_CUSHION

TOP TIP

Why not make multiple cushions to pony-fy your bedroom? It'll look super-cute!

4 When you get about 10cm from where you started, close the stitch and then turn the cushion the right way out.

Ask an adult for help when using scissors or a needle.

TOP TIP
You could upcycle old clothes to make this cushion – it's a great way to help the planet!

5 Use your cushion or soft toy filling to stuff it as much as you can. Make sure you fluff up the filling and push it in gently, then ensure it's evenly distributed.

6 Use a ladder stitch (check out tutorials online for a step-by-step) to close up the cushion – and there you have it – an adorable Valentine's cushion!

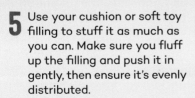

PONY PACES

TRANSFORM YOUR TROT

Make your fave pony hot to trot with our wise ways to perfect this pace!

Some practice working on your pony's straightness, balance and impulsion will do wonders for his trot work. Try our ace ideas and your pony will be showing off his finest trot moves before you know it!

Fancy footwork

Trot is a two-beat pace, in which the pony's legs move in diagonal pairs. The footfall sequence is...
- nearside (left) hindleg and offside (right) foreleg together
- offside hindleg and nearside foreleg together

TOP TIP

Remember your diagonals. You need to be sitting as your pony's outside foreleg comes back and rising as it goes forward.

POSITION PERFECT

Trotting can be done sitting or rising, but we'll focus on rising trot and how your position can influence your pony...
- remember the two straight lines that should run through your body in the saddle – head-hip-heel and elbow-hand-pony's mouth. If you're in better balance, your pony will be, too
- as you rise out of the saddle, think about pushing your hips forward towards your pony's ears. This is because your pony is moving forward, so if you try to rise up straight you'll get left behind his movement and could bounce down on the back of your saddle – ouch!
- as you land back in the saddle, allow the momentum of your pony's trot to naturally push you back up again

EXERCISE ONE

RAISE THE GAME

Riding over raised trot poles means your pony has to work harder and lift each leg higher. Raised poles will help to improve his balance, suppleness, impulsion and expression. Here's what to do...

1. Place five poles on the centre line, set 1–1.2m apart.
2. Using small blocks or pole raisers, lift each pole at alternate ends.
3. Ride an active trot around the arena then make a square turn onto the centre line and ride over the poles.
4. If all goes to plan, keep the height really low but try raising each pole at both ends and repeat!

EXERCISE TWO

CIRCLE IN THE SAND

Not only will this test your accuracy as a rider, but it'll do wonders for your pony's suppleness and straightness, too. So where do you start?...

1. Ride a 20m circle at either B or E.
2. When you get back to your starting point, ride a 15m circle to take you to the three-quarter line.
3. On returning to your starting point again, ride a 10m circle to the centre line.
4. Then, work your way back out to the bigger circles, first a 15m then 20m.
5. Change the rein and do the same the other way!

Fix it - fast!

Your pony might fall onto his forehand in trot and you'll feel this if he pulls on the reins or starts to trip. If this happens, ride loads of transitions from trot to walk to halt, then walk and trot again. You'll soon feel him lighten up!

HOME IS WHERE THE HEART IS

When Owen's told that the livery yard where he keeps his pony is closing down, it's time to go in search of a new one

"**Y**ard meeting!" called Patricia, the yard manager. Owen stopped grooming his pony, Peppa and looked over at his friend, Becky, who shrugged.

"I wonder what this is about?" he asked. Owen popped Peppa back inside her stable and headed towards the tack room. At that moment, his mum pulled up in her car, just in time to join the meeting, too. Once all the liveries were sitting around the tack-room table, Patricia cleared her throat and began to speak.

"I have some unfortunate news," she said. Everyone listened intently. "Hilltop Farm has been sold and I'm afraid the new owners won't be keeping any liveries, so everyone has one month to find somewhere else for their ponies to live."

Everybody gasped and then a gaggle of voices all sounded at once. "But what are we going to do?"

"I don't want to move anywhere else."

"This is the worst news ever!" Meanwhile, Owen sat quietly looking down at his wellies, trying to blink away the tears.

The search begins

On the drive home, Owen stared out of the window while his mum tried to comfort him. "Don't worry, there are some lovely yards around, I'm sure. We just have to look."

Owen loved Hilltop Farm – it was his favourite place in the whole world. It was where he dreamt of being when he was stuck doing boring maths at school. It was the place where he knew everyone and everyone knew him, and it held treasured memories from when he first had Peppa two years earlier.

"But nowhere will be as good as Hilltop," replied Owen, quietly, squashing his cheek with his palm as he leant against the car door.

That evening, Owen's mum scanned websites and Facebook groups in search of any leads, while Owen sulked upstairs in his bedroom. He texted Becky, both

sharing in their misery at the awful news. "I'm going to view a yard tomorrow for Striker, but, apparently, there's only one space," she said. Owen's heart sank. Even though he and Becky saw each other every day at school, the thought of not having her at the yard to ride with and chat to made him feel even more dejected. "But we might not like it," she texted again.

Owen knew everyone would be in the same boat and that all the liveries would be fighting for places at the local yards. There were 12 liveries in total looking to move from Hilltop Farm and only so many vacancies nearby.

> "The horses were immaculate and there was a set of jumps in the huge school"

Not quite right

When Saturday came around, Owen's mum had scheduled to visit a couple of yards that sounded promising. Owen took Peppa on a quick hack with Becky and Striker first thing, but the atmosphere at the yard was strange. Secretly, Owen was still hoping that they might find a new yard together.

After riding, Owen and his mum drove 10 minutes down the road from Hilltop Farm to Lowbridge Fields. Mum said she'd seen a written advert on Facebook and the price sounded fair. However, when they turned up, Owen was already wary. The stables looked in a poor state from the outside and he noticed some barbed-wire fencing in a few of the paddocks.

They were greeted by a kind-looking lady who

was covered almost from head to toe in mud, but her smile took up her whole face. As she showed them around, Owen tried to hide his feelings, but he knew he would never want to take Peppa there.

There were no other children for him to ride with and no school, either, even though there were grass fields for riding in during the summer. He just didn't get a good vibe. Owen's mum said thank you to the lady and that they'd think about it and let her know.

"I hated it," said Owen, crossing his arms as they got back into the car.

"All right, but we've still got one more to see today," his mum replied.

Long way off

Next, they pulled into a yard that was the complete opposite of Lowbridge Fields. There were automatic gates, a beautiful brick driveway and a massive school right by the entrance. Owen's stomach flipped – it was amazing. They were greeted by a young groom who gave them a tour. All the horses looked immaculate, there was a set of jumps in the huge school and even a horse walker! Owen couldn't stop thinking about how much fun he could have with Peppa, using all the facilities to get her in tip-top condition.

"And what are the turnout arrangements?" asked Mum as they walked past the fields, which looked rather small and sparse.

"They have a full day out during the summer from eight until four but they stay in during the winter months to save the grazing," said the groom.

Owen sighed. He didn't want Peppa standing in her stable all winter – so this yard was a no, too.

When they returned to the car once more, Owen shed a tear. "We're never going to find anywhere as good as Hilltop are we?" he said. "What's the point?" Mum put her arm around his shoulders and squeezed.

"Of course we will," she said. "These things always turn up when you least expect them. I'll keep looking and maybe Becky will find somewhere with two spaces so you can stay together?" Owen nodded, but it all seemed so unfair.

A wish come true

A week later, Owen was wistfully mucking out Peppa's stable when Becky came bounding up to him. "Owen!" she said, practically shaking with excitement.

"What?" he grumbled. Becky moved into Peppa's stable with him so she could speak without anyone overhearing. "Guess what!" she whispered. "My dad's cousin is opening up a new livery yard only five minutes from my house! It's a little further for you, but basically there'd be room for everyone here! I wanted to tell you first!"

Owen's eyes widened. "Really? That's incredible!" he said.

"My dad's talking to your mum about it now. We're going to go for a look – come with us?" asked Becky.

Owen, his mum, Becky and her dad drove down to view Willowdown Livery Stables. Becky's cousin, Eleanor, was a qualified instructor who competed in eventing. She wanted to run a livery yard, too, so had started renting Willowdown to run as a business.

Eleanor greeted them when they arrived and Owen liked her instantly. Even though there were only a few of Eleanor's own horses already there, the place somehow felt like home. The wooden outdoor stables seemed airy and light, the fields were a good size and Peppa and Striker could go out as a pair. There was even a school! Could this really be the solution they had all hoped for?

All's well that ends well

A week later, Eleanor pulled into the Hilltop driveway to collect Peppa and Striker and take them to Willowdown. Seven of the other liveries from Hilltop Farm were joining them later in the week. It'd be the same happy crew as before, with a whole world of new adventures ahead of them. As Owen and Becky turned the ponies out and watched them sniff their new surroundings and have a good roll, they breathed a sigh of relief.

Eleanor had sent them schedules for some events she could give them lifts to with the ponies, and the summer holidays were just around the corner. Owen realised it wasn't only the place that mattered, but the people in it, too, and he knew it was just the start of something great.

SPRING

As the clocks go forward and the days gradually get longer, the grass in your pony's field will start to grow more – hallelujah! Not only is that good news for you because it means more turnout time and less mucking out (boring!), but it's also sure to cheer up your pony after a long, cold winter. Seeing him prance around with delight will certainly put a smile on your face, too!

THROUGH

Spring, summer, autumn and winter - there's something to love about each and every season

AUTUMN

Yes, clipping isn't the most glamorous or fun task – cue getting covered from head to toe in pony hair! But having a freshly clipped pony is as good as putting on a fresh, fluffy jumper. That feeling when you run your hands over his velvety coat... bliss – especially if you've given him a hot cloth after so he's shiny all over. Clipping also means rugging and who doesn't love snuggling up with their pony and stealing his heat to warm up their hands?

If you love competing, summer is sure to be full of fun days out with your pony. After all, you've been working so hard on getting him fit and prepped, so why not spend as much time as you can earning those rosettes in the glorious sunshine? If competing's not your thing, visiting your fave equine charity, attending a demo or watching a big event is the next best thing, and summer is the perfect time for those sorts of adventures.

THE YEAR

WINTER

When you get one of those cold but sunny winter days after a few weeks of rain that has meant hours in the saddle have been reduced, there's nothing better than going for a hack with your friends to soak up some winter sunshine. You might get chilly toes, but it's sooo worth it for the gorgeous scenery. Through the ears pics with frosty trees and clear, blue skies – dreamy!

PICTURE THIS

Can you guess all 12 horsey items correctly from these close-up pics?

1 _ _ _ _ _ _ _

2 _ _ _ _ _ _
_ _ _

3 _ _ _ _ _ _

4 _ _ _ _ _ _

5 _ _ _ _ _

6 _ _ _ _ _ _

7 _ _ _ _ _ _

8 _ _ _ _

9 _ _ _ _ _

10 _ _ _

11 _ _ _ _ _ _

12 _ _ _

I SCORED /12

How did you get on?
Check out p101 for
the answers!

FOAL TO ➡️
FULLY GROWN

Discover the five life stages that turn cute little foals into perfect ponies, with our timeline

Who doesn't love a cute, cuddly foal? With their inquisitive nature and enthusiasm for life, they're just the best, right? When a foal's born, there's a lot of growing up to do – mentally and physically – and this happens over several years. To find out exactly how these little bundles of fluff become magical mares, glorious geldings or stunning stallions, stop right here!

1

BABY LOVE

Mares are pregnant for around 11 months, which gives their foals time to fully develop in the womb. Once he's born, a foal's first mission in life is to get to his feet because in the wild he might need to run away from predators. Believe it or not, foals can stand up within a couple of hours of birth! It's thirsty work being a foal, so feeding from Mum is high up on a foal's to do list. This is sooo important because a mare's milk contains colostrum and all the other nutrients foals need to fight off disease and stay healthy.

DID YOU KNOW?

Foals play an active role in their delivery by extending their head and front legs and rotating into a diving position ready to enter the world!

2

TODDLER TIME

During the first few weeks of life, foals will suckle three to five times an hour, even though they'll start to nibble at grass from a week old. After a couple of months, the mare's milk becomes less nutritious so the foal needs to get his nutrients from solid food instead, such as grass and hard feed. Then, when he's four to six months old, a foal will stop feeding from his mum altogether and this stage of a foal's life is equivalent to being a human toddler!

3 CRACKING CHILDHOOD

When a foal reaches a year old, he or she is known as a yearling. At this stage of their life, they're curious and love playing, galloping and running around with their friends. They still need guidance from other horses and humans, though, as they don't know everything about life just yet! During this time, yearlings may be taught to lead in hand and stand quietly for the vet and farrier, or to be groomed. That way, they're easier to handle when they become bigger and stronger!

DID YOU KNOW?

Yearlings and two year olds can look gangly and unco-ordinated, due to their body parts growing at slightly different rates.

4 TERRIFIC TEENS

From two to four years old, male foals (if they haven't been gelded) are known as colts and females become fillies. Equivalent to a human teenager, colts and fillies can be taught to wear a bridle and saddle and respond to voice aids. The backing process, when they're taught to carry a rider, is usually left until the age of three or four when their skeleton is more developed. This process must never be rushed! Backing a pony is a really important life lesson and should only be carried out by an expert. That's why owners often send their ponies to professionals to start their ridden career.

5

AWESOME ADULTS

By the age of four, a pony is almost fully matured and is ready to start his training. Female ponies are now referred to as mares, while male ponies are either stallions or geldings, depending on whether they've been gelded. The world is your oyster when you have a young pony. Whether you want to jump, do dressage, mounted games or simply enjoy hacking around the countryside, most ponies can turn their hoof to anything.

BOOST your CONFIDENCE...

Check out our handy tips that'll make riding in a group a breeze

RIDING IN A GROUP

Whether it's when you're out hacking or sharing the school, the pressure of riding with, or being watched by, others can affect your confidence. But one of the most enjoyable parts of riding is getting to do it with your pals because the adventures and memories are multiplied! Here's how to feel confident riding in a group.

1 FOCUS ON YOU

When you're riding with others, it can be easy to let your imagination run away with you and think that everyone's watching you ride. In reality, they're likely to be far too busy thinking about themselves and their own ponies to be concerned about what you're doing. Try not to be distracted by what's going on around you – fill your mind with what you want to achieve with your pony. Check in with your position from your head to your heels, ride some transitions to be sure your pony is listening to your aids and even try singing a song inside your head to help focus your mind.

2 PICK THE RIGHT PEOPLE

If you're going out hacking with your riding school, you're likely to be grouped based on ability, whereas if you're on a livery yard you might have found friends who are keen to go hacking, but who enjoy a much speedier ride than you do! It's a good idea to plan your route beforehand and ask what paces you'll be riding in so you can make a decision whether it's the right thing for you – there's nothing wrong with taking a rainbcheck if you don't feel up for a canter through the woods just yet. Find people to ride with who respect your confidence levels and you're set up to have fun.

3 COMMUNICATION IS KEY

Speak out if you have any worries. This is super-important if you're going on a fast ride – always ask others to slow or stop if you feel out of control or scared. But it's also important if you're riding in the school and you or your pony are worried by others who are jumping or going faster. It's okay to politely ask them to take a breather while you finish and leave the space safely, and definitely better than staying quiet and risking a confidence dip or, worse, a fall.

4 STAY ON THE BALL

By constantly assessing your surroundings, whether you're in the arena or out hacking, you'll be able to deal with tricky situations as quickly and calmly as possible. While schooling, you'll need to keep an eye out for who has priority over the outside track, for example, because if you're not aware then it could result in a collision! When you're in an open field, however, consider others – for example, dog walkers or cyclists – and ensure you give them plenty of space as well as letting your pony know they're there so he's not flustered by them.

ALL ABOUT TEETH

There are tons of cool facts to learn about your pony's teeth - check them out right here!

CHECKED OUT

Ponies need regular dental checks from a vet or qualified equine dental technician to make sure there are no problems – not only can issues make your pony uncomfy, they can lead to weight loss and difficulty eating. How often a pony has dental check-ups depends on his age and whether he's had problems with his teeth before. Sharp edges are the most common problem found by equine dentists – often caused by uneven wear – and they must be filed down using a rasp to prevent the inside of the mouth from becoming irritated.

COUNT YOUR BLESSINGS

Foals have 24 baby teeth, also known as deciduous teeth, that are totally replaced by permanent adult teeth. On average, ponies have 36–42 adult teeth – this number varies due to the pony's gender and whether they have any wolf teeth – and they'll normally have the full set by the time they're five years old. Sometimes the caps on the baby teeth don't fall out naturally so an equine dentist will remove them.

ON THE JOB

Ponies have different kinds of teeth, just like we do, and they each have a different role. The incisors, at the front of your pony's mouth, are used for cutting the grass as he grazes – and for grooming his pals! The premolars and molars towards the back of your pony's mouth are responsible for grinding up his food before he swallows it.

GENDER WARS

Canine teeth are the short, sharp ones situated in the gap next to a pony's incisors. They're usually only found in geldings, but some mares do have canines. In the wild, a male pony will use his canine teeth as weapons in a fight, but they have little purpose in domesticated ponies today!

A SPARE PAIR

Wolf teeth are the small teeth that sit just in front of the upper and, more rarely, the lower premolars. They usually start showing when a foal is 5–12 months old, but not every pony has them. Wolf teeth come in all sorts of shapes and sizes and owners often choose to have their pony's wolf teeth removed before they cause any problems – due to their position they can sometimes interfere with the bit.

GROWING PAINS

Unlike human teeth, ponies' teeth never stop growing! They're really hardwearing and will grow 2–4mm per year but as a pony constantly chews while he's grazing, he grinds down the teeth's surfaces so they don't grow too big for his mouth.

DARE TO TRY
STUNT RIDING

Doing the unthinkable and breaking all boundaries... see what it takes to be a stunt rider

Ever seen a horse and rider in a movie doing some cool tricks like the horse rearing up or galloping through the woods really fast? That's what we would call a stunt and it uses a special rider for this more dangerous side of acting. The rider usually works as a double for the main actor or as a background extra to perform trickier scenes.

Where to start...

Training any horse or pony to do something requires a lot of patience and repetition so they can understand what to do. The same would go for teaching horses stunts.

When training stunt horses, the trainer will keep the sessions short and allow the horse to learn one trick at a time. They'll start with basic training, getting them to learn something such as picking up a leg when asked. Over time, when the horse has a better understanding and bond with the trainer, he can then learn the really cool stuff like falling down, rearing on command or having someone jump off the side of him while he's still moving – epic!

DID YOU KNOW?

Actors aren't the only ones who use make-up in films, horses do, too! They'll wear animal-friendly make-up to make them appear dirty or injured for certain scenes.

Do you have what it takes?

To be a stunt rider, you need...
- bravery
- flexibility
- courage
- patience

The horses used in movies are super-talented! The most common breeds used are...
- Andalusians
- Friesians
- Thoroughbreds
- Arabs
- Welsh ponies
- Quarter Horses

DID YOU KNOW?

In the original *Black Beauty* movie, five different horses played Black Beauty.

Why not have a go?

Although stunt riding takes years of practice and should not be practised at home without the proper training, you can teach your pony to do cool tricks from the ground! A super-awesome trick to try would be to get your pony to pick up his front leg on command. You can use words like 'leg up' while picking up his leg so he gets to know what you want from him - make sure to give him a tasty treat, too, when he does it right. Try not to be too hard on yourself, though, when it doesn't happen straight away, as it takes a lot of practice and a lot of time - patience is key!

DID YOU KNOW?

Training sessions should roughly be about 30 minutes to keep the horse interested and not overfaced with too much at once.

HACKING HIERARCHY

Feel super-confident hacking in a group with our guide!

If you've ever felt nervous about going for a hack in a group, you're certainly not alone. With unfamiliar objects, open space and several ponies who have minds of their own, it can be a nerve-wracking thought. But hacking with friends is sooo much fun and once you feel confident about going adventuring with your pals, you'll never look back!

INTO POSITION

It's important that your pony behaves no matter his position within the group because if you encounter a problem, you'll be sure that you can control him and get home safely. Plus, being able to ride him in any position with other ponies shows that he...
- trusts you
- listens to you
- feels confident and brave
- has good manners

This means that you'll always have a super-fun hack because you'll feel confident, too!

LEADER OF THE PACK

To be at the front of your group, your pony needs to be sensible, brave and confident. If he's too fast, or nappy or spooky, he might influence others which might make your hack much less enjoyable.

If your pony is bold, he might naturally want to be in front but if he's less brave and you want him to happily lead the way, give him lots of encouragement and take him out regularly with a confident companion.

As the rider, be super-vigilant and on the look out for any hazards lying ahead. Your job is to communicate with the others, telling them when you're going to slow down, asking them if they're happy to speed up and making sure no one gets left behind.

MIDDLE GROUND

If your pony is the nervous type, he'll most likely find being in the middle of the group his favourite spot – he has friends either side of him to protect him! When it's safe to do so, try riding alongside the person at the front to slowly boost your pony's hacking confidence. This will give him the chance to see more while having a friend close by for guidance.

TOP TIP
Always take a fully charged phone with you and make sure everyone is wearing plenty of high-vis.

TAKE A BACK SEAT

To get the most enjoyment out of being at the back of your group, your pony needs to be patient and not pushing his way past the pony in front of you. Being at the back often brings an important role of supporting a nervous pony, and if you let your pony overtake his worried friend, it might knock their confidence.

If your pony likes to go zoomies with his pals, you might find keeping him behind his friends tricky, because he'll want to rush to the front. But it's super-important he learns that he can't always be in front, otherwise he'll always try to take control. If you're struggling to keep your pony at the back, try going on slower hacks to keep the energy levels low, and ride lots of transitions to get him listening to you.

CHANGE OF SCENERY

The great thing about hacking is that there are endless places to explore and a variety of environments to experience. But ponies can act differently depending on the environment around them, so knowing how to ride in these situations will help you enjoy your hacking even more!

OPEN UP

Ponies often get more excited in open spaces, which can be daunting, so before heading out to an open field, make sure you're in control. Ride lots of transitions and work out where your pony prefers to be in the group because this will help keep you safe. As you feel more confident, mix up the position you ride him in so he understands he can't always have his own way.

You can also use the extra energy to your advantage – it might be the perfect time to practise your walk to canter transitions, or leg-yield!

TOP TIP
Try to avoid always cantering along the same stretch of track because your pony will start to anticipate what's about to happen. Mix it up and walk or trot him on your fave gallop spot from time to time.

THE MIGHTY JUNGLE

As you ride through the woods, you might not be able to see what's around the corner, so take it slowly unless you can see a clear stretch ahead of you. Stay focused and alert because the trees can create big shadows and sudden light changes might cause your pony to spook.

The great thing about woodland hacks is fallen trees. Extra XC practice? Yes, please! But always check the ground either side first for any hazards, such as rabbit holes. Watch out for tree roots, too, because they can cause your pony to trip.

TOP TIP

If you come across another rider or group of riders when out hacking, slow down to a walk and allow plenty of space as you pass each other.

HORSEY HIGHWAY

When riding on the roads be super-sensible and extra-aware of everything going on around you. Make sure you're familiar with the Highway Code – there's lots of guidance about the dos and don'ts to help keep you safe.

It's best to stick to walk when on the roads because trotting on hard ground can jar your pony's legs. Make sure you communicate with other road users, too, using signals to tell them when you're turning – and to thank them for slowing down for you. The good thing about getting your pony used to being ridden on the roads is that he'll feel more confident in busier environments such as competitions – winning!

TIME TO TACK UP

Tacking up's a simple task with our easy step-by-step

There are lots of adventures to be had in the saddle, but you need to know how to tack up before hopping on board! If you've not tacked up before, it can be confusing with all the straps and buckles but follow our guide and you'll ace it.

1 STAY PROTECTED

It's important your pony wears a saddle pad to protect his back from being rubbed. Lift the saddle pad over his back and place it so the front is over his withers, then slide it backwards slightly into position – doing this will make sure your pony's comfortable and that his hairs are lying in the right direction.

SADDLE UP

2 Carefully lift the saddle and gently place it on your pad. Using both hands, hold each end of the saddle pad and pull it up towards the saddle so it's sitting clear of your pony's spine – this is to make sure it doesn't cause pressure points. Then, secure the pad straps to the saddle.

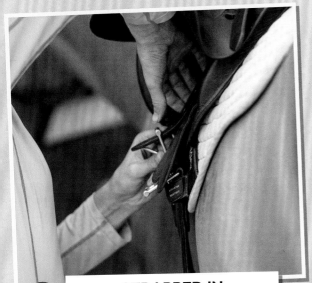

STRAPPED IN

3 Grab your pony's girth and attach it to the straps on one side of the saddle, making sure it's threaded through the girth loop on the pad. Walk around to the other side of your pony, slowly bend down to pick up the girth that's hanging down and thread it through the girth loop on the pad, then fasten it to the straps – don't do it up too tightly to start with and slowly increase the tightness.

TOP TIP

Before you start tacking up, pop on your riding hat and boots, as well as your pony's boots if he wears them, so you can get on and ride as soon as you're ready!

OVER YOUR HEAD

4 Now for the bridle! Start by unclipping your pony's leadrope. Place the reins over his head, clip the leadrope back on and then remove his headcollar. It's a good idea to keep one hand around your pony's head and the bridle over your other arm so you can hang up the headcollar with your free hand.

INTO POSITION

5 Use your right hand to hold the bridle by the cheekpieces and guide the bit in with your left hand – to encourage your pony to open up, try wiggling your thumb against his mouth. Lift the bridle towards and over his ears so it's sitting in the correct position.

BUCKLE UP

6 Gently pull your pony's forelock over the browband and secure all the buckles. Start with the throatlash, making sure you can fit four fingers between it and your pony's cheek. Then, straighten the noseband and secure with two fingers' width.

WELSH PONIES

Get to know this totally epic breed...

DID YOU KNOW?

Welsh ponies are known for being good-doers – this is because in the wild, food is hard to find, which requires them to travel across very hard terrain!

There are four different sections when it comes to the Welsh pony breed. These are Section A, B, C and D and all four evolved to survive the hard rocks and ditches of the Welsh mountains. Although they're tough on the outside, they're super-soft on the inside, and they have a very good temperament – but they're often quite spirited, too!

BREED BIO

Did you know Welsh ponies have...

- ✓ small heads
- ✓ large eyes
- ✓ sloping shoulders
- ✓ short backs
- ✓ strong hindquarters
- ✓ high-set tails
- ✓ coat colours most commonly in black, grey, chestnut and bay

Quick reverse

There is evidence to suggest that the Welsh ponies originated from the prehistoric Celtic pony and was present long before the arrival of the Romans.

Galloping forward to the 19th Century, many ponies were purchased to be used down the pits to pull the trains that transported the coal through the mines.

FUN FACT

In the early 1900s, Welsh ponies were only accepted into the studbook if they could trot 35 miles uphill from Cardiff to Dowlais without stopping. The test took three hours to complete!

Why do they make the best first pony?

Section A – They don't grow bigger than 12.2hh and are the smallest of the Welsh breeds. They have a large eye and a small head with a slightly dished face, features inherited from the Arabian horse. Section As are used for driving, showing and as kids' riding ponies.

Section B – They don't grow bigger than 13.2hh. They're slightly lighter in build as a result of the Thoroughbred and Hackney blood. Nowadays, they're commonly used for riding and are great as hunters or even as jumping ponies.

Section C – Like the Section B, they don't grow bigger than 13.2hh, but they're heavier and more cob-like. They make great driving ponies but are also used for jumping.

Section D – Is the largest of the Welsh breeds and must stand taller than 13.2hh. These ponies cover a wide range of activities, but thrive in the show ring!

Make! CHRISTMAS gingerbread STABLE

Get into the festive spirit with our awesome gingerbread stable!

1 Heat the butter, sugar and golden syrup in a small pan over a low heat. Stir until the sugar dissolves, then set aside to cool.

2 Mix the flour, bicarbonate of soda and spices in a big bowl. Then, crack the eggs into another bowl and whisk. Pour the butter mixture into the flour with the eggs and water. Mix well and then use your hands to bring it together into a ball.

3 Lightly flour your work surface and knead the dough for a few minutes until smooth. Roll out the dough until it's the same thickness as a £1 coin. Using the templates, cut out the shapes so you have all five parts of the stable.

4 Preheat the oven to 200°C and space out the gingerbread shapes on a tray lined with greaseproof paper. Bake for 6–8 minutes, or until golden brown, then leave to cool completely on a wire rack.

Ask an adult for help when using the hob and oven.

Download the templates at **bit.ly/GINGERBREAD_HOUSE**

You'll need...

- ☐ 175g butter
- ☐ 175g soft dark brown sugar
- ☐ 3tbsp golden syrup
- ☐ 700g plain flour
- ☐ 1½ tsp bicarbonate of soda
- ☐ 2tsp ground ginger
- ☐ 2tsp mixed spice
- ☐ 1tsp ground cinnamon
- ☐ 50ml water
- ☐ 2 medium eggs
- ☐ templates
- ☐ a tub of royal icing
- ☐ piping bag
- ☐ sweets and chocolate for decorating!

TOP TIP
Use chocolate buttons to create a realistic tile effect on the roof!

TOP TIP
You might have some spare dough, so why not cut out some Christmas tree shapes for extra decoration?

5 When you're ready to assemble the stable, put your royal icing into a piping bag and pipe along the edges to stick the walls together. Then pipe around the edges of your roof on the underside and place it on top.

6 Now, all you need to do is decorate! You can decorate it however you like and with whatever treats you want, so don't hold back. Then, when you're done, the stable is ready for your fave model pony!

PADDOCK *perfection*

Do you know what it takes to keep your pony's paddock in tip-top condition?

Ponies love spending time in the field – after all, it's where they can do two of their fave activities, eating and playing! Just like you care for his stable, looking after his field is important for his safety, and making sure his paddock stays in fab condition will help keep him happy and healthy. Take our quiz to test your fieldcare knowledge!

Stay hydrated

1. What should you do if your pony's field water is frozen?

- ○ **a.** Leave it – he'll break through the ice
- ○ **b.** Break the ice up and remove it, or give him a bucket of lukewarm water
- ○ **c.** Pour boiling water on it so the ice eventually melts

2. How often should you check your pony's water supply?

- ○ **a.** Daily
- ○ **b.** Weekly
- ○ **c.** Monthly

Fence it

3. Which type of fencing is not suitable for ponies?

- ○ **a.** Post and rail
- ○ **b.** Electric fencing
- ○ **c.** Chicken wire

4. How often should you walk the perimeter of your pony's field to check the fencing?

- ○ **a.** Daily
- ○ **b.** Weekly
- ○ **c.** Monthly

Penned in

5. What's the most important reason for poo-picking your pony's field?

- ○ **a.** To control worms
- ○ **b.** To make it look tidy
- ○ **c.** To stop him eating it

6. How often should you poo-pick your pony's field?

- ○ **a.** Daily in summer, monthly in winter
- ○ **b.** Weekly all year round
- ○ **c.** Depends on the time of year, the size of the paddock and how much turnout your pony is getting

Under cover

7. Which one of these is not a suitable type of shelter?

- ○ **a.** A large tree or hedge
- ○ **b.** Horsebox or trailer parked in the corner
- ○ **c.** Purpose-built shelter

8. When should you check your pony's field shelter?

- ○ **a.** Weekly and always after a storm
- ○ **b.** Every day
- ○ **c.** Only when he moves to a new field

Totally toxic

9. Which one of these plants is not poisonous to ponies?

- ○ **a.** Ragwort
- ○ **b.** Cow parsley
- ○ **c.** Foxglove

10. How should you deal with poisonous plants you find in your pony's field?

- ○ **a.** Dig them up from the root and ask an adult to burn them
- ○ **b.** Cut them with scissors
- ○ **c.** Ignore them – ponies don't like the taste anyway!

Muddy mayhem

11. Which one of these is not a suitable option for dealing with muddy gateways?

- ○ **a.** Fencing off muddy areas
- ○ **b.** Putting down grass mats
- ○ **c.** Keeping your pony in his stable all winter

12. What time of year should you harrow, fertilise, reseed and roll your pony's field?

- ○ **a.** Spring
- ○ **b.** Summer
- ○ **c.** Winter

I SCORED / 12

How did you get on? Check out p101 for the answers!

PONY PACES

CONQUER THE CANTER

Add power and balance to your pony's canter with our simple advice

Struggling with your pony's canter or simply want to make it even better? Either way, we can help. Read on to find out everything you need to know about cantering and how to ace this pace in no time.

Fancy footwork

Canter is a three-beat pace, in which the footfall sequence is...
- outside hindleg
- inside hindleg and outside foreleg together
- inside foreleg

TOP TIP

Having some lunge lessons with your riding instructor is a great way to develop a deeper canter seat.

POSITION PERFECT

Cantering some ponies can be super-bouncy, so it's important you sit well to make things more comfortable for you both. Here's what to consider...
- sit up, look up and keep a contact with your thumbs on top of the reins
- keep your legs really relaxed and hanging down by your pony's sides – try not to grip with your knees
- to help you sit deeper and more comfortably, imagine you have a piece of paper between your seat and the saddle – don't let it escape!

Fix it - fast!
Does your pony keep breaking into trot? If so, you're not alone. If it's safe to do so, try getting up off his back into a forward seat, ride large in canter around the arena and push your pony on. Do this in both directions several times a week and you'll soon find your pony's balance improves no end – result!

EXERCISE ONE

MAKE THE DISTANCE

This exercise will help you create more 'gears' in your pony's canter, which will help his balance.

1. Place two poles down one long side of your arena, slightly in from the outside track, at least 20m apart (you don't need to set them at a specific distance).
2. Once you've got your pony into a good, energetic canter, ride over both poles and count out loud the number of strides he takes between them. Remember not to count the stride over the first pole!
3. Come over the poles again and see if you can ride one stride fewer in between them. You'll need more energy to do this so your pony lengthens his stride!
4. Successful? If so, see if you can do the opposite and ride one extra stride than you did on your first canter through the poles. This means you'll need a bouncier canter, with your pony taking shorter steps.
5. Repeat on the other rein.

EXERCISE TWO

CANTER-TROT -CANTER

Transitions are a great way to improve your pony's balance, obedience and suppleness, and this exercise can help you do just that!

1. On a 20m circle, pick up canter and ride half a circle.
2. Next, make a trot transition. If your pony loses balance, half-halt to rebalance, and then ask him to canter again.
3. Repeat the exercise a few times, going from canter to trot to canter again, with just a few steps of each pace.
4. Do the same in the other direction!

THE GREAT ESCAPE

Kayla goes on a brave mission when the ponies at the yard go missing

"Good boy, Prince," I said, as my pony lowered his head to let me brush his forelock. "Are you almost ready?" called my friend Abby, as she did up her pony Smokey's girth ready for our hack. Late as usual, I made my way to the tack room to gather my equipment and within five minutes I was ready to go.

Abby and I loved hacking every Saturday, and we ventured through the local woods and snuck a canter along a grassy bridleway, laughing with glee. On our way home, we cooed over the ewes and their lambs in the fields opposite. They looked adorable, with their wagging tails and springy step. "Who's that?" I said, narrowing my eyes. In the distance, I could see a man dressed all in black staring in our direction with binoculars. "Seems a bit strange..." mused Abby. "Maybe he's bird watching?" The man seemed to notice we'd caught sight of him and quickly retreated into a four-wheel drive car. We said goodbye to the lambs and continued riding home.

Raise the alarm

The next morning, I woke up at the crack of dawn to the sound of Mum calling me from downstairs. "Kayla, come here, quickly!" My stomach flipped and I threw on my dressing gown and flew down the stairs. "We've got to go to the yard right now. I've just had a call from Patricia – the ponies have escaped!" I felt all the blood drain from my face. What if they were in danger? I put my wellies on over my pyjama trousers and Mum and I jumped into the car.

We met Pat and the other liveries at the yard, where they were collecting buckets full of treats and headcollars ready to find the ponies. "Have there been any reports of where they've gone?" said Mum.

"Someone online has put that they've seen a horse wondering down Frenchman's Lane, but that was a little while ago now," said Pat. Abby emerged from one of the stables and I could tell she'd been crying. I ran over and gave her a hug, assuring her that we'd find the ponies – even though I didn't know if I believed it myself. Over her shoulder, I heard the parents talking in hushed voices.

"How did the horses get out?" asked Abby's dad.

"I found their field gate wide open and the chain lock had been cut," said Pat.

"Do you think they could've been... stolen?" I heard Mum ask.

"Let's not jump to conclusions," said Pat.

The search is on

Some of the adults went in their cars to search the roads, but me and Abby decided to go on foot with Abby's dad in case they'd gone down one of the local bridleways. I hoped they hadn't ventured onto any busy roads. We were looking for four horses in total, Prince, Smokey and their two older field mates Benson and Denzel.

"Prince! Prince!" I called out into the bright morning haze as Abby and I wondered along the bridleway we'd been on the day before.

"Smokey!" called Abby, in between sobs.

"Wait, shh, I hear something," I said. We both froze and so did Abby's dad.

I could hear a noise coming from across the field. I narrowed my eyes as they focused through the mist and I could see a silhouette running into the distance. "There's someone there!" I whispered. Then I remembered the strange man from our hack. Could it be him?

The three of us crept along the bridleway but we couldn't find an entrance to the field. "I think there's a cut-through here," said Abby. We crouched down and tried to get a closer look at what was happening. As we got nearer, I saw that there were two men loading sheep into a trailer attached to a Land Rover. "Is it the farmer?" said Abby.

"I've seen the farmer when we've been out hacking and that definitely doesn't look like him!" I said, thinking hard.

Luckily, the sound of the sheep loading onto the trailer covered our tracks as we legged it back to Abby's dad, Peter, who was already on the phone. "We think they're stealing the sheep!" said Abby a little too loudly, and we all ducked in case we were seen. "I'm calling the police," said Peter.

and the man spun around. Prince towered above him, rearing up to full height. The man let out a low scream and scarpered back to the car. The two of them jumped in and drove away, while Prince pawed the ground and sniffed me. I burst into tears and hugged his neck.

Caught red handed

Flooded with relief at finding the ponies, I quickly slipped on his headcollar. Then, I was able to call for Abby and her dad, who helped me catch the rest and lead them back to the yard. Luckily, they were all safe and sound with no injuries, but we called the vet to check them over anyway. The police even managed to track down the vehicle we'd described and stop the thieves in their tracks, so the sheep and their lambs could be returned. Prince was a total hero for saving me and I couldn't be happier to have him back.

> " I went to run back up the track as he came towards me, but my pyjama top was caught on a bramble "

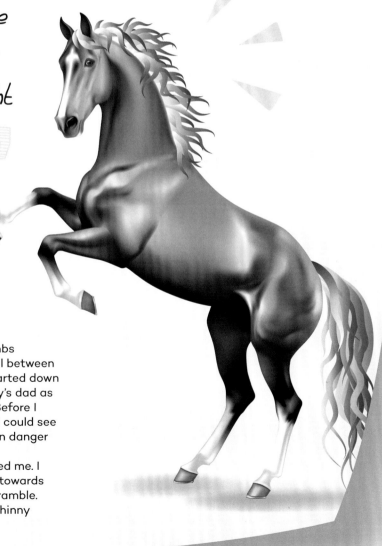

A clean getaway

With the police on their way, our mission was back to finding the ponies. Where could they have gone? There were still no updates from the rest of the search party. Just then, I heard a thundering of hooves and a snort from across the field that sounded like a pony. Prince? I stared again at where the men were – they'd loaded almost all the sheep and lambs by now. Then, I saw a definite swish of a tail between the trees. It was him! Without thinking, I darted down the track towards him. "Kayla!" called Abby's dad as quietly as he could, but I wasn't listening. Before I knew it, I was right by the Land Rover and I could see the ponies in the trees. What if they were in danger and the men tried to steal them, too?

"Hey!" called one of the men. He'd spotted me. I went to run back up the track as he came towards me, but my pyjama top was caught on a bramble. Just as the man got close, there came a whinny

READY FOR RUGGING

Learn how to rug your pony up with our helpful guide

With so many rugs on the market and loads of individual differences to consider, choosing a rug to put on your pony can be tricky. Luckily, our easy guide will help you pick the right rug and show you how to put it on safely!

1 THE BIG DECISION

There are lots of factors to consider when deciding what rug your pony will wear, including the temperature, his access to shelter and forage, his body condition, whether he's clipped, his age, breed and level of work. First, check the temperature on your phone, then visit **bit.ly/RUG_GUIDE** to work out which rug will be best – don't forget to think about the other factors that'll affect your pony!

2 GET DRESSED

Once you've decided which rug to put on, fold it in half so it's inside out then give your pony a little scratch on the neck and talk to him so he knows something's about to happen. Carefully place it on your pony so the front of the rug is just over his withers. Gently unfold the back half of the rug, making sure it sits centrally along his back.

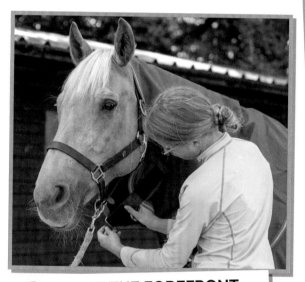

3 AT THE FOREFRONT

Check the rug is sitting just in front of his wither – if it puts pressure on his wither, it'll be uncomfortable and restrict his movement. Then stand by his shoulder and fasten the chest and neck straps. Make sure all the Velcro is fully covered to stop it getting dirty and, if the rug has buckles, that the straps are tucked into their keepers.

TOP TIP

If you're not sure which rug your pony needs, it's best to ask someone for help and if you're stuck between two, go for the lighter option because it's easier for ponies to warm up than cool down.

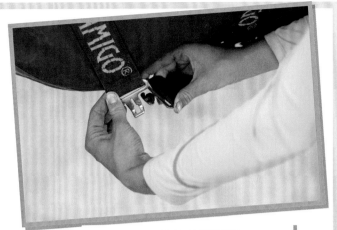

4 CRISS CROSS

Secure the belly straps, also known as surcingles, by crossing them under your pony's tummy. It's a good idea to put one hand on your pony's side as you reach down, and do it all efficiently and quietly to prevent him from being spooked.

5 FASTEN YOUR SEATBELT

Walk towards your pony's hindquarters and, standing to the side of him, carefully lift his tail over the fillet string. Some rugs have two leg straps instead of surcingles – to fasten them, pass the first one around your pony's hind leg and clip it onto its hook on the same side, then as you repeat with the second strap, thread it through the first one so they interlock to help keep the rug in place.

6 GET A FEEL

Once your pony's been wearing the rug for a little while, gently slide your hand down his neck to feel how warm he is. It can be really helpful to make a note of the weather conditions and the rug he was wearing, so you get an idea of which rug to choose next time.

RIDE THE *perfect...* DRESSAGE TEST

Check out our tips that'll help your dressage scores skyrocket!

You don't need a pony with extra flashy paces to achieve high dressage scores, as long as you crack the basics of rhythm, suppleness and accuracy you're sure to wow the judges. There are loads of different movements involved in a dressage test, but follow our six steps and you'll be on your way to achieving top marks!

SET THE SCENE

When it's almost time to start your test, walk and trot your pony around the outside of the arena until the judge signals for you to start. This gives you the chance to show your pony the boards (some ponies find them spooky) and get him focused. It's important that you're ready on time because you might make a silly mistake if you rush!

TOP TIP
If you go wrong in a dressage test, the judge will signal to let you know. Don't panic! Stop your pony and listen to the judge as they'll tell you where you went wrong, then take a deep breath and start from the movement before the one where you went wrong.

FIRST IMPRESSIONS COUNT

Every dressage test starts with a centre line and it's the first chance you have to impress the judge, so make it count! Give yourself plenty of room to turn onto your straight line and focus on maintaining it all the way to C, where the judge will be sitting. Remember to keep your head up and smile – after all, competing with your pony is fun, so try not to let your nerves get in the way!

During your training get a friend to video from C to see how straight your line is. You could even use poles to help channel your pony while practising! As you ride down the centre line, think about sitting in the middle of the saddle and keeping an even rein contact.

AROUND THE BEND

Riding a smooth turn around the corners of the arena will do wonders for your marks because it shows that your pony is balanced and supple. If your pony tends to cut the corner, it's likely that he's rushing and isn't bending through his body. If this is the case, focus on slowing him down using a half-halt and press with your inside leg to encourage him to bend as he travels around the corner. Take care not to ride too deep into the corner, though, because this could disrupt his rhythm and balance so the test will become less fluid.

ON YOUR MARKS

It's not just the accuracy of your movements that make up your score, you'll also get marked on your riding, as well as your pony's paces, impulsion and submission. He should be working over his back freely, have regular paces and a desire to work actively. He should also be responsive to your aids.

It's important you take time to work on your aids – they should be clear and concise – and your position, too. Remember that your shoulders, hips and heels should be in a straight line!

TOP TIP
Once you've finished your test, reward your pony by giving him a scratch on his wither. Then walk on with a loose rein to allow him to stretch and leave the arena at the A marker.

Take time to work on your aids and position

LOOP THE LOOP

It's likely you'll ride serpentines, circles or half circles in your test, so they're worth finessing so you can guarantee a fab score! The size of your circle and each loop of your serpentine needs to be super-accurate, and to achieve the perfect circle or serpentine, your pony needs to be supple on both reins and maintain and change bend in his body.

In your training sessions, measure out the different shapes and use markers to help guide you, then gradually take them away to test your accuracy and aids. Can you still ride the same shape perfectly? Remember to turn your upper body, keep your eyes up and encourage your pony to bend through your seat and legs, rather than by using your reins.

SQUARED UP

The halt at the end of your test is the last chance for you to show off yours and your pony's skills to the judges, so practise whenever you can! To achieve a square halt, your pony needs to be balanced and working from his hindquarters. So, in your training encourage him to work actively from behind and just before you halt, squeeze on your reins slightly and sit deeper into your saddle to keep him in balance. Avoid pulling on the reins and leaning forward because that will load his weight onto the forehand. Keep practising your halt and immobility (when your pony stands still for at least three seconds) and you'll be nailing it in no time!

ON THE RUN

Last Saturday my best pal, Louis, had a lesson with his sharer, so our time in the field was cut short. But Sunday funday was just around the corner and, boy, did we have a good time in the field that morning. The grass was green, the sun was shining and we had the whole day in the field... or so we thought. The thing is, we were playing 'tag' – basically chasing each other around – and we got a little sweaty from the zoomies. Louis isn't as fit as I am, so he was dripping when his owner unexpectedly turned up to bring him in and ride. She was less than impressed! Oops!

Ronald

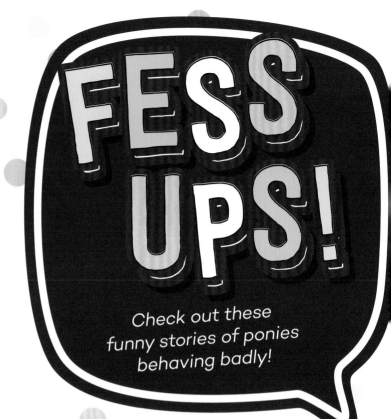

FESS UPS!

Check out these funny stories of ponies behaving badly!

STITCHED UP

When the warm sunshine is beating down on my back, I always feel super-calm and relaxed. Today, despite being gloriously sunny, was different, I don't know what came over me – I must've slept well last night because I had so much energy! Jess, my owner's friend, keeps her horse, Pete, in the same field and he loves to play, so when I'm in the mood for playtime, he's always raring to go. We got a bit carried away, though. I momentarily forgot he was wearing a fly rug, grabbed it with my teeth, pulled too hard and practically ripped it in half! I'm going to be in so much trouble – my owner's going to have to buy Pete a new rug! Sorry!

Milo

LET LOOSE

I'm prone to laminitis so unfortunately, I'm stabled more than I'd like, but it's for health reasons and my owner, Jake, is good at helping me break the boredom. I have stable toys to keep me busy, a radio playing my favourite station and windows to look out of. However, one day Jake must've been in a rush because I didn't get my hay ball. I was feeling a bit bored, so I put the time to good use and learnt a new trick – how to open my stable door bolt! I'm not interested in running away, but Jake's face whenever he sees me standing there with the door open is a hilarious sight!

Lady

CRINGE-O-METER

Waaay cringe!   Wasn't me!   Kinda cringe!

PIG OUT

I know I'm not popular when I run away whenever someone comes to catch me but I just love food and I'll take any chance I can get to munch on some extra grass. Emily, the rider for my afternoon lesson, was aleready running late and when she eventually caught me, she made me trot all the way down from the field – exhausting! She tied me up when we got onto the yard and ran off to get my tack. Silly Emily, though – she didn't tie the quick-release knot correctly and I untied myself. Cue me wandering over to the lushest patch of grass (it was too good to resist!) and sending Emily into a panic when I wasn't where she'd left me!
Tinks

HEADS UP

I recently moved to a new home where the stables are in a big, open barn and have low walls so I can say hello to my neighbours. It feels so nice to be able to mutually groom my new friend, Knight, from the comfort of my own box – it also means he can't steal my food, so it's the best of both worlds! But I have discovered a problem with my stable in particular. Now, I'm not the smallest horse – standing at 17hh some would consider me tall – and that's not convenient when the barn also has low beams. Every time I poke my head over to see Knight, I bash it on the wooden beam. Will I ever learn to be careful?
Frazzle

SLIP 'N' SLIDE

I'm off to a fancy comp tomorrow, the National Championships apparently! I live in the field 24/7 and my owner, Sam, always tells me when we're going to a show so I don't roll the night before – I've got to stay clean for him! But today, I think I got overexcited because I was running around in delight and slipped over. Luckily, the ground was soft, so I wasn't hurt but I did slide through the muddiest patch – disaster! Hopefully, Sam won't be disappointed in me tomorrow morning.
Diego

LIVING THE *dream*

What's better than a whole day at the yard with your pony and pals?

Whether it's at the weekend or during school holidays, getting to spend the whole day at the yard is always so exciting! And if you're pony-mad it's likely to be at the top of your priority list – but what's involved in the perfect yard day?

In the saddle

No matter if you prefer to ride on your own or enjoy having company, riding is likely to be the main part of your day, so why not come up with a plan for your session? Deciding what activity you'd like to do will make it mega-productive and ultra-fun! Discover an epic hacking route with the perfect place for a canter, come up with a musical ride and show it off to your parents or set up a funky grid to boost your pony's technique!

Chit chat

The yard is the perfect place to make like-minded friends – you'll probably end up finding a life-long bestie and spending all your spare time together! But whether you're catching up on the week's events, planning your next horsey outing or just having a giggle, being with friends is so good for your mental health – plus, with ponies involved it's the best thing ever!

Spa day

It's the ideal time to give your pony a mega pamper session! He'll feel so loved and will be sparkling from head to toe once you've given him a thorough groom and bath. Make him feel fab with a massage, scratch on his fave itchy spot and a stretching session, too.

Spring clean

There are loads of other horsey tasks that require time and effort and a day at the yard is the perfect chance to get them done. It could be essential things like cleaning your brushes, getting rid of stable cobwebs or polishing your tack. Or perhaps you could organise your numnahs, tidy the tack room or repaint the jumps!

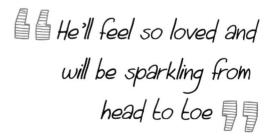

He'll feel so loved and will be sparkling from head to toe

Get competitive

Desperate to compete your pony but don't have access to transport? You could organise a yard competition day for everyone to get involved in! Whether it's in-hand showing, gymkhana games, showjumping or dressage, find out who's keen to get involved and create a fun schedule for the day. You could even find prizes for the winners of each class!

Check it off

Do you dread sweeping the yard or checking fencing? Why not do all your important yard chores with a friend? It'll make them so much more enjoyable if you have company, so they won't feel like a bore! You'll probably be more productive if you have a little help, too, which means you can enjoy a longer ride or grooming sesh!

New adventures

With hours to spare, why not go exploring or try an activity you've never done before? You could watch how your pony behaves in the field, go for a bike ride while your friend turns her pony out, grab a basket and go fruit picking in summer, or take your pony for a picnic – the options of fun things to do are endless!

TOP TIP
Don't forget to take a packed lunch with you so you can stop for a refuel halfway through the day!

TOP TIP
If you're now dreaming about the perfect yard day, why not message a friend and get a date in the diary for some fun? You won't regret it!

THE MISADVENTURES OF CHARLIE!

Charlie grows his own parsnips

THE ANNUAL 2024 FUN

ALL ABOUT THE ANNUAL

How much have you learnt from your annual? Take our quiz to find out

1. What strong material are hooves made from?

....

2. What's the height range for a Highland pony?

....

3. How many beats are there in each walk stride?

....

4. How long can an archery track range from?

....

5. What can you do to keep your pony focused in the cross-country start box?

....

6. How many Exmoor ponies were left after the Second World War?

....

7. What age is a pony almost fully matured?

....

8. What is the name for the teeth at the front of your pony's mouth?

....

9. What pair of legs move together in canter?

....

10. What does every dressage test start with?

....

SPOT THE DIFFERENCE

Can you find these pictures in the annual and spot the two differences in each one?

TURN OVER FOR MORE ANNUAL FUN

STABLES SUDOKU

See if you can put one of each symbol in every row, column and 3x3 box!

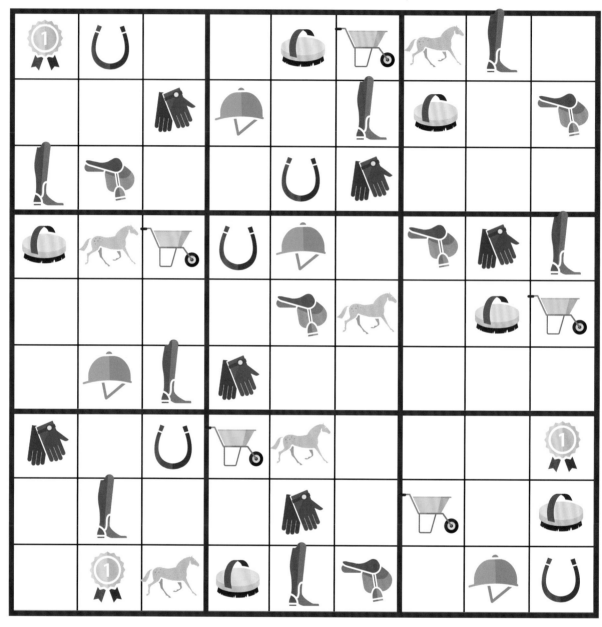

HOW DID YOU GET ON?

To check your answers, scan the code or visit
bit.ly/PNY_QUIZ_ANSWERS

QUIZ ANSWERS

WHAT'S YOUR WORKPLACE? P28

Mostly As
Your creativity could see you becoming an **equestrian journalist** or working in a **horsey marketing role**. Not only do you love reading and writing, but you're a socials guru and there's nothing better than posting up pony videos online, right? Maybe, one day, you might find yourself working in the PONY mag office – how cool would that be?

Mostly Bs
With your attention to detail you could find yourself becoming a health expert, and the options are endless. Could you see yourself as a **vet**? Or maybe a **physiotherapist**, **saddle fitter** or **nutritionist**? There's no doubt about it, horses' and ponies' wellbeing is your top priority and you're a firm believer there's no such thing as too much knowledge.

Mostly Cs
Guess what? You have what it takes to be a **riding instructor** or even a **professional rider**! How amazing would that be? Your determination and love for riding will go a long way towards helping you achieve your goals, but remember to be kind to the horses and ponies you ride and train along the way. Their welfare should always come first.

Mostly Ds
With your practical head and physical skills you'd make a brilliant **groom**, **equine dental technician** or even a **farrier**! You're a hands-on person and a real grafter, always the first to help out. These jobs might be long hours and hard work, but you'll welcome any challenge and give it your best shot.

COAT OF MANY COLOURS P42

Mostly As
You love grey ponies most. Your personality colour means you're positive and optimistic and your pony will pick up on that, too. You're a wise, independent spirit who appreciates the simple things in life and you like things to be neat and tidy.

Mostly Bs
Chestnuts are your preferred choice and this means you ooze energy. You're witty, generous, spontaneous, optimistic and bold, and you and your pony have sooo much fun together. You're a real problem-solver and sometimes your imagination runs wild.

Mostly Cs
Black ponies are your fave and the colour symbolises someone who's never afraid to go after what they want. You're determined and strong-willed, and you like to stay in control of your pony.

Mostly Ds
You've got a soft spot for the golden coat of dun ponies. The colour gold means you're loyal, organised, dependable, thorough, sensible, punctual and caring – phew! A loving and compassionate person, you make ponies feel relaxed and valued.

PICTURE THIS P54

1. Shavings fork
2. Jump cup
3. Stirrup
4. Body brush
5. Kick bolt
6. Rug
7. Riding boot
8. Hay
9. Air jacket
10. Bit
11. Plaiting bands
12. Hoof

PADDOCK PERFECTION P76

1. b
2. a
3. c
4. b
5. a
6. c
7. b
8. a
9. b
10. a
11. c
12. a

0-4 points
Uh oh, you're a **field foe**! Try learning more about paddock maintenance by watching videos online, reading PONY mag and asking your yard manager – you'll be climbing up the ranks soon!

5-9 points
Good job, **field friend**! You have a great baseline level of knowledge on field care, but just try to pay a little more attention to the finer details and you'll be a field fanatic in no time!

10-12 points
Woo hoo, you smashed it **field fanatic**! Your pony's in the best hands when it comes to looking after his paddock because of all your awesome knowledge! Congratulations!

Jump with no hands — **4**

Do around-the-world — **1**

Jump a water tray or spooky filler — **7**

Canter one lap without stirrups — **2**

Complete your next dare with jockey stirrups — **9**

Swap ponies and jump a cross-pole or ride a serpentine — **6**

DARE TO BE

Spice up your schooling session with some super-fun riding challenges!

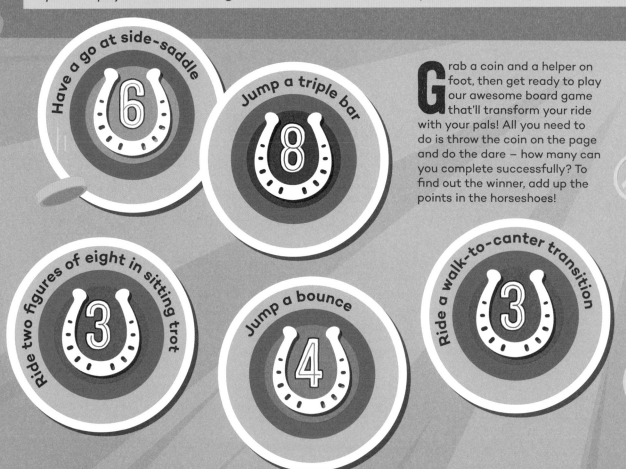

Have a go at side-saddle — **6**

Jump a triple bar — **8**

Grab a coin and a helper on foot, then get ready to play our awesome board game that'll transform your ride with your pals! All you need to do is throw the coin on the page and do the dare — how many can you complete successfully? To find out the winner, add up the points in the horseshoes!

Ride two figures of eight in sitting trot — **3**

Jump a bounce — **4**

Ride a walk-to-canter transition — **3**